GET MUDDY

GET MUDDY

PERSONAL STORIES
OF
OBSTACLE COURSE RACING

GAIL WAESCHE KISLEVITZ

BREAKAWAY BOOKS
HALCOTTSVILLE, NEW YORK
2015

Get Muddy: Personal Stories of Obstacle Course Racing
Copyright © 2015 by Gail Waesche Kislevitz

ISBN: 978-1-62124-019-8
Library of Congress Control Number: 2015945485

Published by Breakaway Books
P.O. Box 24
Halcottsville, NY 12438
www.breakawaybooks.com

FIRST EDITION

CONTENTS

INTRODUCTION

Who are these people who run obstacle courses? What's it like? And why do they want to roll around in mud, crawl under barbed wire, jump into containers of ice water so cold you gasp for air, jump over fire pits and through tear gas, or risk electrocution from live wires hanging down all around them? "Because it's more fun than running a 5K," says Sharon Remy of Florida. Since 2011 she has competed in obstacle course races—commonly referred to as OCRs—such as Tough Mudders, Warrior Dashes, Savage events, and the new kid on the block, BattleFrog. Her kids have completed their first BattleFrog youth event. Remy is just one of millions to embrace OCRs, which are sweeping the country and the world. And there is already a push to make it an Olympic sport. Before you shake your head at that, remember that snowboarding was once a cult craze and is now an Olympic sport.

Everyone from couch potatoes to ultramarathoners and Ironman finishers is embracing the obstacle course racing phenomenon. What was considered a fad just a few years ago is now the fastest-growing sport in US history, expanding at an exponential rate, especially among women, since the first OCR exploded on the scene in 2009. To put that in context, the first New York City Marathon was held in 1970 with just 127 runners. It took forty-three years and two running booms for the New York City Marathon to reach a field of fifty thousand entrants in 2013. Running USA reported that there were 541,000 US marathon finishers in 2014. In comparison, Obstacle Race World, a website that tracks the sport, estimated that five million people completed an obstacle course in 2014.

OCRs vary in length and time, but usually range from 3.1 to 13.1 miles, and most can be completed within one to six hours. There can be several hundred to several thousand participants at any given event. A typical entry fee ranges from $60 to $200, with team registrations usually receiving a 5 to 10 percent discount for each entrant. Spectators have to pay up as well to see their friends or loved ones get creamed on the course. And everyone signs a death waiver.

The money is pouring in. Everything from shoes to climbing ropes to gyms is being customized to meet the growing demand for obstacle course racing. You can buy branded clothing for your race or take an OCR cruise. Spartan Race held their first OCR cruise in 2014. At Tough Mudder events, participants can get a free tattoo (at some events) and a free Mohawk haircut. Tough Mudder has brought in $70 million in revenue since hitting the scene in 2010. The OCR industry is now well over $250 million and growing.

And there is prize money. Max King, a thirty-five-year-old running elite from Bend, Oregon, cashed in a $30,000 check for winning the inaugural Warrior Dash World Championship in October 2014. King's cash haul was part of the race's $100,000 purse and was by far the largest prize he's won as a competitive athlete. At the Tough Mudder fourth annual world championship in Henderson, Nevada, the winner earned $60,000, another sign that obstacle course racing is growing at a torrid pace in the United States.

So who are these people and why do they get muddy and put their bodies through torture? On average, they range in age from twenty-five to forty—but that can span from fourteen to ninety. The gender ratio is sixty–forty men to women, but women are coming on fast with races of their own like the Dirty Girl Mud Run and Mudderella events. Participants range in fitness level from sedentary couch potatoes who don't bother to train to endurance athletes who train every day.

They include Katie Day, forty, from Mahwah, New Jersey, who gained and lost the same sixty pounds for years until she joined a fitness program and finally kept the weight off. A friend at the gym suggested they do a Tough Mudder. "I did it as a whim," says Day. "It looked like fun on YouTube." But it wasn't that fun. The electrical wires felt like "sticking a finger in a electrical socket and having your legs buckle under." By the time she finished, she was so exhausted that she wanted to hire someone to drive her home. She swore she'd never do another one. Since then, however, she has embraced the sport and completed another Tough Mudder, a Warrior Dash, and a Rugged Maniac. She recruits friends to join her and displays her finish-line photos on her office desk.

They include Louis Vazquez, fifty-five, from Brooklyn, New York, a former 2:36 marathoner who got tired of chasing mile after mile in the marathon and was looking for a change. He did his first Tough Mudder in 2010 and has become obsessed with OCRs, forgoing all marathons. His goal now is to complete a Spartan Beast. For Vazquez, the thrill of an OCR is the element of surprise, the unexpected obstacle that is always a part of the course. "In a road race, you know what is involved. It's the next mile and the next. Nothing new," he explains. "I liked the idea of not knowing what was next."

It's people like Mike Johnson, thirty-two, from Memphis, Tennessee, a former NFL football player currently completing his oral surgery residency. He claims that completing his first Tough Mudder was the scariest thing he has ever done. He trained like he was back in football camp and looked forward to the physical challenges after being on call for thirty-six hours or operating on trauma patients.

And it's kids. Most OCR organizers include a kids' event, a shortened, age-appropriate course for kids ages four and up. On the Spartans of the Northeast Facebook page, you can learn how to turn a typical backyard swing set into a Spartan training center for your tot.

Vazquez, Day, and Johnson are just some of the people you will meet in *Get Muddy*. Their stories will inspire you, make you laugh or cry, or leave you impressed with the gritty ways they overcame seemingly insurmountable obstacles and changed their lives. Summing up the allure of OCRs, Denise Mast, international quality manager for

Spartan Race, Inc., says: "For the most part, people who complete an OCR change their tune from *I can't* to *I can* and apply that to their everyday life. It transforms them."

But I think there is something else going on here as well. People choose to do an OCR for many reasons. Some are personal, some are therapeutic, some involve ego—like accepting a dare to appear manly. I believe they fill a fundamental ache we all experience at some point in life to break out of a void in a way that doesn't take five months of training, like a marathon, and isn't as daunting as, say, climbing Mount Everest. OCRs are doable; in fact, some people don't even train for them. They are different, they're fun, and they make you feel like a kid again. They are welcoming. Participants feel they belong to an engaging community of like-minded people. And just like marathons before them, OCRs are becoming the hip, new place to drop on one knee and ask for your loved one's muddy hand in marriage.

If your life needs a reboot for whatever reason, an obstacle course race could be the ticket.

THE BIG THREE EVENTS

Spartan Race Series

Spartan Race was created with a simple mission in mind: to get people back to their primal roots, doing what they were designed to do—run, jump, climb, and sweat. Most of the courses are held on ski slopes or other hilly terrain.

Joe DeSena and Andy Weinberg created the Death Race in 2005. It's an insane event that attracts just a few brave souls. It continues for up to seventy hours through the woods and hills of Pittsfield, Vermont, and only 10 percent of the field of no more than two hundred finish. The Spartan Race series was created in 2010 to bring the excitement of obstacle racing to everyday athletes who can actually start and finish the race. Spartan offers three levels of events, three-plus miles (Sprint), eight-plus miles (Super), and twelve-plus miles (Beast), each filled with mud, water, and signature obstacles. They are held throughout the United States and franchised to fourteen countries including Mexico, Canada, many European countries, South Korea, and Australia. In

January 2013, Spartan Race entered into a partnership with Reebok as its event title sponsor, creating the Reebok Spartan Race Series. Spartan races are timed events.

According to Denise Mast, international quality manager for Spartan Race, "Obstacle course races are basically elements of play, the fun things we did as kids that we don't get to do anymore." She adds: "Finishing an OCR can truly transform a life, turning a couch potato into an athlete. The last runner of the day still gets the cheers and medal that the winner received."

Spartan offers youth races that encourage kids to jump, run, get muddy, help one another, and have a good time while conquering obstacles. They are age-appropriate, starting at age four.

Spartan is also very encouraging to women with the Spartan Chicked program, which includes a closed network on Facebook with more than five thousand participants.

Spartan recently formed a charity fund-raising partner, Everydayhero, a platform for participants to raise both money and awareness for those in need. Participants can choose to fund-raise for one of the forty charity partners registered with Everydayhero or for a personal cause.

Warrior Dash

Warrior Dash is the obstacle course race that anyone can start and everyone can finish. With more than fifty international locations and over two million participants since 2009, Warrior Dash has reinvented the concept of a 5K run and created a revolution: Warrior Nation. Elite athletes and novice runners alike conquer twelve world-class obstacles like Goliath and Great Warrior Wall, wade across wooded lakes, and venture through mud-caked back roads to cross the finish line. Participants are rewarded with a finisher medal that doubles as a bottle opener and magnet, a T-shirt, a fuzzy Warrior helmet, and ice-cold beer. At the post-race party, Warriors relive the course with friends, dance to live music, and celebrate the decision to leave their normal weekend in the mud.

An industry pioneer in the experimental entertainment industry, the first Warrior Dash was held in Joliet, Illinois, in 2009 and sold out at two thousand participants. The following year Warrior Dash launched its first nationwide obstacle race series and, based on that success, went international in 2011. Warrior Dash does not have a kids' event but is open to ages fourteen and above.

The first Warrior Dash World Championship took place in 2014 in Esparto, California. Its parent organization, Red Frog Events, has committed to raise $25 million for St. Jude Children's Research Hospital. According to Lauren Gardner, operations and public relations manager, "Warrior Dash is the event that anyone can start and finish and feel a sense of accomplishment. It's the gateway OCR."

Tough Mudder

Tough Mudder started out as a submission for a Harvard Business School competition by Will Dean in 2009, and has grown into a thriving enterprise. Will Dean and Guy Livingston, the Harvard students from England who came up with the idea based on a UK event called Tough Guy established by Billy Wilson in 1987, are now heading up an $80-million-plus corporation with over a million and a half confirmed Mudders. In 2015, Tough Mudder will hold more than fifty events globally.

A Tough Mudder is an untimed, team-oriented, ten- to twelve-mile obstacle course event. As the website states: "A Tough Mudder is not a race, it's a challenge that puts teamwork and camaraderie over finisher times and rankings. A vast majority of our obstacles require teamwork and communication to overcome." Finishers receive the coveted orange headband. Legionnaires are repeat Mudders who collect multiple headbands and wear them all at one time.

Really tough Mudders can compete in the Tough Mudder World Championships, which put the world's most hard-core Mudders through a twenty-four-hour challenge with double the obstacles per mile of any other Tough Mudder event. Unlike other Tough Mudder events, World's Toughest Mudder is a competition, with three official categories designed to find the toughest man, woman, and four-plus-person team. Cash prizes are awarded.

Tough Mudder supports Wounded Warrior Project. To date, they have raised over $6 million for service members returning home with the mental and physical wounds of war to assist them on the journey toward a successful civilian life.

MELINDA AND ERYK COLLINGS

Port St. Lucie, Florida

"It changed our lives."

Self-described overweight couch potatoes, Melinda Collings, thirty-three, and her husband Eryk, thirty-eight, had just returned from a trip to the Caribbean and were showing photos of their vacation to friends. When Melinda saw herself in her bathing suit on the big screen, she was horrified. "You can forget just how fat you are until you see yourself in a different light," she says. That was their wake-up call for getting in shape. They quit their pack-a-day cigarette habit, joined a gym, and eight months later entered a Warrior Dash that changed their lives.

Melinda and Eryk laugh when asked if they were active growing up or participated in sports. "I tried out for sports teams but was never picked," says Melinda. Eryk played golf but describes it as driving around in a golf cart drinking beer and smoking cigarettes. They were both twenty-year smokers. They did odd jobs to make a living. Melinda worked at call centers, wove trapeze safety nets, and is now a software developer. Eryk worked as a bike mechanic and was a DJ at a nightclub, which is where he met Melinda.

They married in 2003, when she was just twenty-one to his twenty-seven. One thing is constant about the couple: They love to have fun and enjoy life. They married in Las Vegas at the Stratosphere Casino and Hotel. "It was crazy and wild and fun, like us," says Melinda of their wedding. Over the years, their weight slowly climbed, Eryk getting close to three hundred pounds. Their diet was mainly Hamburger Helper, mac and cheese, and fast food. They both drank two or three 2-liter bottles of Mountain Dew a day. By the time they took their vacation in 2011, they were pretty much couch potatoes. But after seeing themselves in those photos, they had an epiphany.

As Melinda states: "You don't realize how things can get out of hand when you are not paying attention." Eryk adds: "When you look in the mirror every morning and it is just you in that image, you get used to it and don't see yourself for what you are: overweight and out of shape." They were so out of shape that they couldn't hike up a hill to catch a stunning vista of the island where they stayed. "I was so disappointed in ourselves," says Eryk. "We had to stop and rest, we were so out of breath. We never made it to the top."

After that night of showing the photos, they speak of their lives as BWA—before Warrior Dash—and AWD—after Warrior Dash. They decided to join a gym, but first Melinda went online and found Warrior Dash. "I thought that could be our goal," she says. "It seemed like we could do it, and more importantly it looked like a lot of fun." The next morning they walked into a gym, hired a personal trainer, and told him they wanted to do a Warrior Dash in eight months. As fate would have it, they picked the right trainer. He had never done an OCR but knew about them and researched the best ways to train for one. Instead of keeping Eryk and Melinda inside the gym and training them traditionally, he took them outside and had them carry logs and cement blocks up and down the street. He took them to playgrounds and worked on the monkey bars. He had them hopping over obstacles in parking lots, running up and down hills, flipping tires. "He was amazing," says Melinda. "We actually looked forward to going to the gym."

Melinda and Eryk made sacrifices to reach their goal. Money was tight, and a personal trainer was certainly not in their budget. They canceled their cable TV to pay for the trainer. They changed their diet, stopped drinking soda, and ate healthier meals. "It took a lot of determination to do this," says Eryk. "It wasn't easy but we knew we had to do this for ourselves." In the eight months, Eryk's pants size went from a 42 to a 36. By the time he did the Warrior Dash, his weight was down to 215.

They signed up for the 2012 Warrior Dash in Clermont, Florida. After all their training, they felt prepared but scared. To test themselves, they ran a 5K and were pleased that they didn't have to stop.

Melinda went online and researched the obstacles they would face. Despite her homework, they still made rookie mistakes—like wearing cotton T-shirts instead of the wicking kind, along with crappy, worn-out sneakers rather than trail running shoes—thinking it wouldn't make a difference. The morning of the event brought the worst weather possible. "It was raining, thundering, bolts of lightning, and it was cold, thirty degrees," says Melinda. "It was gloom and doom and we were soaked from the start." But they were determined and were not put off by the weather.

The obstacles looked daunting but they quickly learned that if they gave it their all, they'd succeed. "We were definitely out of our comfort zone, but what we love about Warrior Dash is that every obstacle is doable if you just try." At five foot two, Melinda was tested by the wall obstacles but conquered them all. And she adds with her typical enthusiasm, "How can you fail when you are having so much fun?"

The second-to-last obstacle was the fire jump, followed by the mud crawl. "When we crossed the finish line we were covered from head to toe in mud," laughs Melinda. They finished in 50:22 and were thrilled with themselves. Eryk's first thought upon finishing was, *It's over? Really? I want to do more!* Melinda felt the same way. "We had worked so hard to get to this spot and now it was over. I was actually sad! But then we got to party . . . and Warrior Dash throws the best party ever."

That first Warrior Dash changed their lives. Since 2012 the Collingses have participated in ten more OCRs and have entered the running and triathlon scene. Melinda runs half-marathons, 10Ks, and 5Ks. Her favorite new thing to do is GoRuck events, defined as putting weights in a backpack and going for a long walk while along the way carrying logs or rocks or other fun tasks. Melinda does the longer versions—more than twelve hours of rucking.

After their personal training contract was complete, they joined CrossFit, which is more suited to their new lifestyle. Eryk was so taken with CrossFit that he became an instructor. He also does triathlons and competes in open-water swims. Both Melinda and Eryk are so busy with events, they need to keep a spreadsheet. And along with their day jobs, they are now full-time students getting college degrees. They've managed to keep the weight off and continue to eat a healthy diet. And they never went back to using their cable TV, something Eryk is especially proud of. "Who needs it! We're too busy to watch television."

They continue to have fun at their OCRs, dressing up in costume and getting friends to join them. Their passion for OCRs and their newfound lease on life is contagious. Warrior Dash thinks so, too, which is why they were invited to be filmed at one of their Warrior Dash events; the results can be viewed on YouTube.

The Collingses have embraced obstacle course racing with a passion and can't imagine their lives without it. They also can't imagine why it took them so long to get to this place—but being wise souls, they realize that the journey to getting fit starts with a wake-up call. It can't be pushed, and it can't be someone else's journey. Their lives are full. They have found a balance that allows them to enter athletic events almost every other weekend, stay fit enough to complete them, finish their homework toward their college degrees, and, as Melinda says, "Eat the occasional cheeseburger!" Now, that is a full life.

VICTOR COTTO

41, Howard Beach, New York

"Next time I'll train!"

You would be hard-pressed to find a family closer than the Cottos. Victor, his wife Celinda, and their daughter Desi do everything together and watch one another's backs. Loyal, at times argumentative and stubborn, always hardworking, the Cottos have a lot of laughter and love in their daily lives. Victor and Celinda are first-generation Puerto Rican and, like most families in their culture, live near their parents and are close with their siblings. Victor is one of eight brothers and sisters. Their parents worked hard to give them a better life and education. But being active and healthy was not part of their growing up. His mom was big on takeout. "Monday was White Castle, Tuesday was Chinese, another night we made white rice, corned beef, and eggs," says Victor of his family's eating habits.

He grew up in the Bronx, playing the usual pickup games with friends. But his favorite pastime was hanging out with his dad, a fireman, at the station house where he was the chef. "Since I was thirteen, I was helping my dad with the cooking," says Victor. "It certainly beat eating all the takeout at home!" After high school, some of his family thought he should enter the army, but Victor had other plans. He wanted to be a chef.

Now working at St. John's University as a sous chef, and previously at AIG (where he was working at the time of the race), Victor has always put in long hours standing on his feet, eight to ten hours a day. In 2013, he needed surgery on his right foot due to bone spurs. "My shift is usually 9 a.m. to 7 p.m., but that could change to 8 p.m. Or I'll have to come in early and work 8 a.m. to 10 p.m.," he explains.

So why would someone who is on his feet all day and rarely gets enough rest sign up to do a Spartan Sprint? "I was challenged by Celinda's brother, who is totally buff," says Victor. His Puerto Rican pride wouldn't let him say no: "I didn't want to be like a wimp." The other member of their three-man team was his brother-in-law Jerry, a New York City policeman. Victor sums up his teammates: "One does obstacles every day as part of his workout and is in amazing shape. The other is a cop who is always working out, running, and outside. I'm a chef who spends all day inside standing on my feet. That's about the extent of my daily exercise."

Victor decided he'd better do something to get in shape, so he chopped down a tree. "Okay, I'm ready!" he said. But even he had to agree that might not be enough. With two months to go, they went to local parks and ran on soft turf, relying on weights at home for strength training. Desi, who was signed up for the Spartan Kids event, used her tricycle for training.

He started going to his local YMCA and ran on the treadmill. Actually, the Cottos try to get to the YMCA on nights or weekends when their schedule allows. Victor and Celinda try to stay in shape to be good role models for Desi. "We take her the Y with us and put her on a treadmill between us," says Celinda. Desi is also on her school's youth running team and enjoys going to the races and winning ribbons and medals.

Victor's event was the 2011 Spartan Sprint in Tuxedo, New York. The night before the race, he lay in bed psyched, anxious, and totally pumped for his big adventure. All he wanted to do was finish. It took them two and a half hours to drive to Tuxedo on race morning. When Celinda first saw the hill that would be Victor's course, she said to herself, *Oh my God. This is going to be a long day!*

As Victor and the guys walked to their wave start, they saw others who had already finished in waves before theirs and were celebrating in the food tents. *Why are they so muddy and dirty?* Victor wondered.

What am I getting myself into? They did a few pushups as a warm-up, said good-bye to Celinda, Desi (who was six at the time), her seven-year-old cousin, the wives, and Jerry's eighteen-month-old in a stroller. This had turned into a big family affair. Celinda was sure it was going to be a momentous day in Victor's life, and she wanted to capture it on camera and press it into her memory.

At the start, they pumped one another up with well wishes and macho bravado, then at the sound of the horn took off running up the hill. Halfway up they got slammed with the fog machine, then got blasted with ice water followed by smoke. Victor struggled to stay upright and running, but when he saw Celinda's brother make it to the top and then run back down to check on him, he was motivated to run harder. "Despite falling and scraping my knees on rocks, stumps, and gravel, I was not going to back down," he states. "I had my pride and was not going to get picked up by the sag wagon. Oh no, not me."

After reaching the top of the hill, he did a body check. Once he'd thankfully seen he was all in one piece, he continued on. "I started running down the hill real strong through the next set of obstacles, thinking like I was Spartacus from the movies. It felt real good for a while and then the fun was over," he recalls. "I had to carry a bucket full of rocks back up the hill and down, then carry a tire back up the hill and down, then crawl through a tire suspended in air, run through the woods, more water, more fog, climb a rope, jump through a tunnel and into a pool of ice water—and that was only halfway!"

By now, he was physically and mentally exhausted. He collapsed on the ground. "I just lay there and thought I was going to die. I thought I would never see Celinda and Desi again. I told the guys, who came back for me, to just leave me there to die," says Victor.

He recovered with some motivation from his brothers-in-law and carried on, but things just got worse. At the Spear Throw, he threw it wrong and the spear ended up grazing his cheek. No blood, but he did stumble, tripping over the stack of spears and almost falling on his face. "I never threw a spear before. How the heck was I supposed to know what to do with that? I'm from the Bronx," he laughs. Then there were the monkey bars, the Horizontal Wall Crawl, and more wall jumps. "I made them all," he says with pride. But before he could finish, he had to face the Barbed Wire Crawl.

"This was one of the worst," he recalls. "I crawled on my belly through mud, rocks, and whatever else was in there, trying to avoid the wire and doing a pretty decent job until the girl in front of me got stuck. When she released the wire, it sprang back into my neck. That really hurt." When he made it through, he realized he was bleeding on his neck, back, and legs from the deep gashes the wire had left.

The guys kept coming back to check on their teammate and offer their help and support, but Victor waved them off. "Just leave me! I'll make it," he told them. He dug deep to find that last bit of energy to finish. Other participants kept passing him as he dragged along. When he noticed others who appeared heavier or more out of shape passing him, he got angry, found his fourth gear, and picked up the pace.

Finally he saw the finish line and was elated—but first he had to jump over a wall of fire, about twenty feet wide and two feet tall, a long block of flaming wood. That was kind of fun, probably because he knew he was almost finished. What he didn't know—and the guys, who had finished and come back to cheer him on, were not about to tell him—was that the finish-line chute was actually the last obstacle, the Gauntlet. Celinda and Desi were also there to see him finish and were a bit nervous about what Victor was heading into.

The Gauntlet, a common Spartan Sprint obstacle, features Spartan employees standing on each side of the finish line chute holding rubber jousting sticks, trying to knock down the tired and wobbling participants. It's also on a downhill. "I never saw it coming," says Victor. "Three huge men were just waiting for me. I made it through the first two but the last one swung hard and whacked me under my knees and I went down hard, and continued rolling down the hill. I thought that hill would never end!" He was very thankful for the hay bale that stopped his rolling descent.

Celinda watched her husband get whacked and roll. "For some reason it struck me so funny, I got hysterical even though I knew he was probably hurting. It was just such a weird and funny sight." Victor had a smile on his face as well, so she knew he wasn't too shaken up. He was smiling because he knew it was finally over.

His first words upon finishing were: "I'm never doing that again!" The second words: "Where's the food tent? I'm starving!" As famished as he was, though, he was too tired and in too much pain to eat. Celinda agrees: "He was really messed up. I felt really bad for him."

To get some downtime and try to recover, Victor and Celinda went to watch Desi and her cousin do the kids' Spartan race, a popular new event. It was a half-mile course with pint-sized obstacles.

Kids climb over mini walls, through tunnels, and get muddy. Desi loved it. An accomplished runner, she took to the course but, like her dad, came away scraped and bleeding. "My baby got hurt!" cried Celinda. But Desi, like her dad, is a trouper and beamed at her accomplishment. She keeps her Junior Spartan medal in her room with her other ribbons and medals from running. Victor hung his finisher's medal in his closet along with his culinary school awards. "We are just one big Spartan family!" says Celinda, obviously proud of her husband and daughter.

Victor relaxed on Sunday but on Monday had to go to work and stand on his swollen feet for eight to ten hours. "I didn't make it through the day," he admits. "I was just too beat up and tired."

Looking back, Victor feels the experience showed him how hard he could push himself to succeed. "This was the toughest thing I have ever done in my life, a true challenge, and I liked that. I've never been out of my comfort zone before, and this really took me out of my element," he says.

"It certainly helped to have my brothers-in-law there to push me. But I am not a quitter and would never have given up, not even when I was lying on the ground saying my prayers."

Celinda feels the experience changed him. "I see it at the YMCA when we work out. He's more into his fitness routine and pushes himself just a little bit more. Before this, he would rush through the workout just to get it over with or try to compete with me," she says. "Now he really thinks about what he is doing, and he is getting better results."

That may be because Victor is thinking of doing another OCR. "Now I know what to expect. It will take more than chopping down a tree to get ready for the next one."

KATIE DAY

40, Mahwah, New Jersey

"I had no idea what I was getting into."

When Katie Day decided on a whim to enter her first obstacle course race with a few friends, they watched YouTube videos of various OCR events and thought it seemed fun. Everyone was laughing and rolling around in mud. It looked like a great way to spend a morning. But she didn't laugh during her first event, a Tough Mudder, in November 2011. In fact, it was "really crappy," and when she finished vowed she would never "f-ing do that again." She's now an OCR addict and loves them.

Day was never a runner. In high school she played tennis and volleyball; she was an all-around average athlete through her college years. But after college she slowly gained weight, steadily moving up the scale from 120 pounds to 190. "I gained and lost the same sixty pounds for years," she laments. She got engaged and joined Weight Watchers to lose weight but ended up calling off the wedding. She stuck with Weight Watchers, however, and lost the weight. She then joined a specialized gym to get fit. "I was determined to keep the weight off," says Day, a very goal-oriented person. "It's easy to gain it but hard to lose it." She wanted to build strength and tone her body and was very dedicated to her routine. While working out at her gym she met a friend who on a whim suggested they do a Tough Mudder. "I didn't even know what that was, but I'm up for just about anything so I said yes," recalls Day.

The event was four months away. They geared up for it by concentrating on running and continuing to work at the gym on upper-body strength. They focused on running trails to get used to that terrain, which is what the Mudder course is all about. They met on Saturdays and ran through the local mountains, building ankle strength and agility. They weren't doing this with an eye on improving their times; instead they just kept up a maintenance routine. They looked at online OCR sites to get tips on what to wear and settled on Nike Dri-Fit shorts and tops.

Day recalls every detail of that first Tough Mudder as if it was yesterday. It was freezing out, thirty degrees at 5 a.m. with a windchill. "Driving down to Englishtown, I was sick to my stomach," she says. "I was so ill prepared for what lay ahead. My first thought was that this was going to be a really crappy day." After taking the Mudder pledge, they were off. The first big obstacle was the Chernobyl Jacuzzi: jumping into a Dumpster filled with ice water. "When I saw this on YouTube, I laughed," she says. "But I wasn't laughing when I had to do it. I stayed cold for the entire four hours it took to finish. It was horrific." Every obstacle included mud, water, and more mud.

At one obstacle, she had to drag herself through muddy water for almost a quarter mile, then climb out of the water by pulling herself up a rope, something she'd already conquered at her gym. Then the only way back was to jump off a platform. "There was no way I was jumping into that water," she recalls of the scary moment. She refused to jump in and ran around the lake, an option. The next obstacle was the Berlin Wall, a series of twelve-foot walls that had to be scaled. After lots of pushing and pulling in delicate areas, she was over the walls. Then more mud: the aptly named Kiss of Mud, in which she had to crawl on her belly through mud and under barbed wire. Finally she could see the finish, but not before one last obstacle, Electroshock Therapy. As she stood at the beginning trying to find her courage, she watched a marine drop and fall after being shocked. By now she had shooting pains down her leg and a severe backache on top of still being bone-cold.

She set out into the obstacle and got nailed. "It was like sticking your finger into an electrical socket and getting jolted," she describes. When she finished, she announced to anyone in hearing range, "I am never f-ing doing that again." She limped to the car and had someone else drive her home, she was so tired.

But she signed up to do another one six months later.

Why? After suffering all that abuse? "Looking back, we had so much fun. We're still laughing about that first one. To be honest, after I got warm and ate steak at our celebration dinner, it didn't seem all that bad." What she loved was the camaraderie, the support from everyone on the course, and the challenge. For the next one, though, they made sure to choose a warm month.

For her next Tough Mudder, she recruited people from her job as well as a few she'd participated with in her first event. They picked a team name—Dixxx and Chicks—and put it on their team T-shirts in orange. They didn't train; in fact, they approached the race with a more carefree attitude than the previous one. "First, it was warm, a real positive, and the terrain was a golf course so not a lot of ankle-biting running," says Day, explaining the course in the Pennsylvania Poconos. More than ten thousand participants were also there. Despite the warmer weather and easier terrain, Day didn't like it as much as her first. "The element of surprise was gone so it was just running to the next obstacle, not as fun. I liked not knowing what was next," she explains.

Day went on to do two more OCRs, a Warrior Dash in 2013 and

a Rugged Maniac in 2014. She loved the Warrior Dash for the fun of it and finished in forty-five minutes, exclaiming at the end, "Holy shit! We're done!" Then the party started. She keeps her medals and race-day photos proudly on display in her office. Even the Dixxx and Chicks T-shirt is on display. With her fine sense of humor, Day has really enjoyed getting into ORCs as way to stay in shape, keep off the pounds, and have fun all at the same time.

MISTY DIAZ

30, Long Beach, California

"Testing my limits and realizing I don't have any."

Since walking her first 5K in 2012, Misty Diaz has completed ten half-marathons and countless other road races at the 5K and 10K distances. She's also gotten into obstacle course racing in a big way, completing five Spartan Trifectas including the Sprint, Super, and Beast—in 2015. For Diaz, who was born with spina bifida, a developmental congenital disorder that involves malformations of the lumbar and sacral areas, every race is a testimony to the fact that she can do anything she sets her mind to. "When I was born, my organs were outside my body and my spine was open," says Diaz, who has undergone twenty-eight surgeries to get to where she is. "Doctors told my mother that I would never walk or eat on my own and that she should abort me," she adds with the conviction that she is a person to be taken seriously. Her accomplishments are also a testimony to her own perseverance and that of her mother, and a wake-up call to her doctors not to give up on anyone.

Diaz grew up lonely, spending most of her life in and out of hospitals and being homeschooled in high school. "Attending school was difficult," she explains. " I was always being pulled out for surgeries and fell behind. Plus I was the only one in my school with a disability so it wasn't easy for me." But it was the only life she knew so it was her normal. Her mom constantly pushed her to overcome her disability and do things on her own. When she did attend school, she rode the bus with all the other kids. Trying to fit in, she used humor and joked with her friends that she walked like Herman Munster.

Despite her attempts at fitting in and using humor, she was in constant pain and by age twelve was addicted to her medications, more than twenty pills a day. By twenty-five she knew she had to change her life. She moved to Long Beach with nothing but $1,000 in her pocket, her car, and her dog. "That was the lowest point for me. I wanted my life back," she says. She slowly weaned herself off most of the drugs and is now down to one. She decided to get healthy and started walking everywhere. She joined a gym and started running on a treadmill, gripping the handrails to stabilize herself. Since she had been walking with hand crutches from the time she could stand, her upper body is impressively strong, whereas her legs have no strength at all, her right leg literally dragging on the ground.

She still remembers the day she was walking downtown and saw a sign for a Ronald McDonald House Walk for Kids. "I knew I had to do that," she recalls. "Ronald McDonald House helped my mom and me a lot when I was going in and out of the hospital all the time." For the families of kids facing serious medical issues, this organization offers a place to stay and meals for extended visits. Diaz and her mom were on a fixed income and greatly appreciated the help. When she completed the 3.1-mile walk, she had an epiphany: If she could walk 3.1 miles, she could run it.

Two weeks later, on April 21, 2012, Diaz ran the Seal Beach 5K. "I didn't have any training, I just signed up and did it," she says. "That race changed my life." She wore a purple tutu, cotton shorts, and non-running shoes from Payless. "I didn't even know running clothes existed," she laughs. "I bought a CamelBak for my water supply and carried a bag of survival food. I was so clueless." It took her ninety minutes to run the 5K, but she finished and drank all her water and ate all her food. She was amazed at the cheers and support she received from spectators who didn't even know the name of the tiny girl with the hand crutches dragging her legs along. "It was an amazing sense of accomplishment and for the first time in my life I felt empowered," says Diaz.

Now smitten with road racing, she wanted to get better and go longer. She entered 10Ks and soon set her sights on a half-marathon, 13.1 miles. But with little to no income, she struggled to pay the race fees as well as the travel costs. She also needed to purchase specialized running gear such as gloves to protect her hands from gripping the crutches for long periods of time and a constant stream of new running shoes, because her foot drag wore them out quickly. She also desperately needed a coach, all of which cost money she didn't have. In 2013, Diaz applied for and won an $800 grant from the Challenged Athletes Foundation to help offset her costs.

With a newfound confidence, she signed up for the September 2013 Yonkers Half Marathon in New York, without knowing that the race is one of the toughest half-marathons in the country. When the race director found out about Diaz's disability, he called her to ask if she knew what she was getting into. As she recalls: "He was so sweet. He called me and hesitantly, so as to not embarrass me, asked me if I knew anything about the course, how difficult it is." She had no idea but like the fighter she has been her entire life, she replied, "No problem." When she arrived the day of the race, the race director was so taken with her chutzpah that he gave her a bib with #1 on it. When she crossed the finish line almost four hours later, he greeted her with a bouquet of roses.

Her race achievements began to appear in her local paper in Long Beach, and she became something of a local celebrity. Diaz was amazed at the support. She also heard from families with children who had spina bifida and reached out to them. "I just want them to know that they should never give up. I understand what it's like to have your mind and heart in constant battle to keep your feet going."

She decided to up her game with obstacle course races. "I really didn't know much about them, but I knew I had a lot of upper-body strength," she recalls when asked why she decided to enter the world of OCRs. "I didn't know how tough they would be for me. I did what I always do and told myself I'll figure it out when I get there!"

For the Yonkers Half, Diaz worked with a coach, Michael Ainis, who had read about her struggles and offered his help free of charge. Ainis also works with Weeple Army; once Diaz told him her plan to do an OCR, he knew he could get a lot of team members to come out and support Diaz.

The day of the Malibu Sprint was not typical Malibu weather; it was twenty-seven degrees. As Diaz stepped out of her car into the cold, she thought, *What am I getting into?* To make matters worse, she stepped right into a huge pile of mud. "I was scared out of my mind." But then the members of Weeple Army embraced her and brought her into their tent. "I never felt so welcome," says Diaz of her new friends. The Weeple Army, led by Dave Huckle, stood by her side and got her through the course. "I won't lie, I was miserable," laughs Diaz. "I was cold and muddy but at the same time happy because of the support I received. They made me laugh." She was pushed and pulled over numerous obstacles but could also rely on her upper-body strength to get over some of them without support. By the time she finished, she was hooked.

"I love half-marathons," she explains of her obsession for OCRs, "but it doesn't compare. Spartan racing is a whole different game. It's totally a mental game; you have to push fear aside and take the next hurdle, without knowing what's waiting for you." Her next event was a Spartan Super. When she saw the course for the first time, she said to her coach: "Are you for real? You want me to climb up those hills?" She completed it and set her sights for a Spartan Beast.

She trains with Coach Michael but also does a lot of workouts on her own. She crosstrains by kayaking, skateboarding, and climbing trees for upper-body strength. She is so dedicated to her training that she's been known to show up at the gym with an IV in her arm.

Diaz has a tattoo on her forearm, a quote from the actor James Dean: "Dream as if you'll live forever. Live as if you'll die today." When asked whether she's in pain while doing an obstacle course race, Diaz responds, "After twenty-eight surgeries this is easy." But not wanting to sound smug, she continues: "I struggle just like anyone else but I embrace the pain as good pain. It means I'm alive and living my life to the fullest."

She continues her thought: "We sign up for these events knowing it's going to be hard, and that we might feel some discomfort, probably pain, and it will take a lot from us to accomplish. Yet we still sign up and train . . . that's pretty badass!"

Diaz is more than thankful for the support she has received from nonprofits like the Challenged Athletes Foundation. She encourages and helps others with spina bifida to get out and enter obstacle course races. "I want kids and adults with spina bifida to feel a sense of accomplishment, to be proud and excited just like I [am]. I want them to know anything is possible, if you have the will." Indeed: Diaz holds two obstacle course race world records for adaptive athletes.

To get a sense of Misty Diaz and everything she has accomplished, go to any of her YouTube videos and be ready to be amazed. And then look at her smile and know that this girl has the world on a string.

EVA ROSE DWYER

34, Manhattan, New York

"Once I make the commitment, I never quit."

According to the Tough Mudder website, "Tough Mudder is not a race, it's a teamwork-oriented challenge that puts camaraderie over course time." A lot of teams are made up of family members, co-workers, or other like-minded groups looking to spend a few hours together in mud, ice pools, and obstacles that include live electrical wires, challenging one another to complete the course. Eva Rose Dwyer, thirty-four, a marathoner, convinced her family to join the ranks of Tough Mudders. They completed the 2012 San Diego Tough Mudder as Team "Boom Goes the Dynamite" and had a blast doing it.

Dwyer is never one to quit, not even when in excruciating pain. Like the day she ran the 2008 Chicago Marathon. She trained well and was looking to qualify for the Boston Marathon with a time of 3:30 or better, but things didn't turn out that way. With one month to go, she came down with a knee injury. She tried every physical therapy treatment available, including ultrasound, deep tissue massage, and arnica shots directly into the knee. Her parents had already bought the plane tickets to cheer her on so there was no backing down. Not that she would. She's not that kind.

As she recalls the marathon, "The first half wasn't so bad. But I was doomed for the entire second 13.1 miles. I could barely run at all." She lost four toenails and was in severe pain. But she couldn't disappoint her parents, so she sucked it up and finished in 4:10. That's the kind of person she is.

Dwyer grew up in South Kingstown, Rhode Island, the second of five siblings. They are all very close to one another and to their parents. They enjoy doing things together. She ran cross-country in junior high school and was always an active kid. Her father, Dave Dwyer, a chiropractor, joins his kids in their racing adventures. In 2011, he joined Eva Rose on her Hood to Coast Relay team, sleeping in the van and blending in very well with the eleven other thirty-something sweaty, tired, but fun-loving teammates. He's also run five marathons, two with his daughter Robin. Her mother, Joan, is the official photographer and cheerleader for the family adventures.

It was no surprise to anyone who knows Eva Rose that eventually the idea of doing an OCR as a family would beckon. According to Eva, it was her prompting that got the family talking about it. She was done with marathons for a while, losing her motivation due to all the injuries. But she also needed a goal and a challenge to keep things interesting: "I tend to be the type of person who does really well with goals and with a team. I'm not quite as good on my own and was looking for the next thing."

The next best thing was the 2012 San Diego Tough Mudder. "This was just the right distance for me, " recalls Dwyer. "Thirteen miles with some obstacle courses thrown in sounded so much better than training for a marathon." She corralled her father, her sister Robin, Robin's boyfriend (now husband) Brandon, her other sister Amelia, and Amelia's boyfriend to form a team. They all thought this would be a fun "badass" challenge. They chose San Diego because Robin was already living there and it was February and they thought it would be a nice break from the northeastern winter; she'd heard that Tough Mudders in the cold can be really nasty. They bought race entries for one another as Christmas presents in December 2011. The only downside was that her two brothers, who were in college at the time, couldn't join them.

With two months to go, they did some training but made a pact that this was going to be for fun and not a race. Basically, they winged it. Part of the Tough Mudder mantra is that it is not a race, but a challenge, and they embraced that element. "We all had our individual strengths and weaknesses and felt that as a group we would pull each other through it," recalls Dwyer.

She didn't do any CrossFit training or weight strengthening; she ran, and that was all. An email chain was started to find a team name and T-shirt design. The emails set the tone for the team and the way they approached the event. "We did a lot of trash-talking and suggested some really funny names," recalls Dwyer. They also picked nicknames. Hers was Eva Wazam. "Our trash talk was really about how incredibly unprepared we were," laughs Dwyer.

When they arrived in San Diego two days before the event, a bit of humorous panic set in. Dwyer remembers the anxious chatter in the car: "What are we doing here? What do we wear? What are we in for?" They met some people who had done a few Tough Mudders and got some tips such as taping their socks and pant cuffs to seal out the mud and covering their knees to protect them from all the crawling. They also studied the website for the possible array of obstacles they could face.

The morning of the event they drove an hour to the start. "We weren't stressed out, but there was definitely some giddy nervousness," says Dwyer. "I remember looking at the course and saying, 'Eek, I actually have to do this!'" The course was eleven miles and included twenty-three military-style obstacles. After signing the death waiver and paying $10 for their mom to come on the course, they posed for lots of badass photos, giving their best Tough Mudder stance. Then it was off to the wave starts.

At the starting line, all "Mudders" pledge to help their fellow Mudders complete the course and leave no Mudder behind. They listened to the speeches, intended to pump up everyone with chants such as, "You are tough! Go get it!" Then they were off, charging straight up a hill. Within fifteen minutes some were walking, some were still running, some wished they were back home.

Dwyer's team regrouped and decided that they were going to stay together; the weakest link would set the pace. The first obstacle was scaling a twelve-foot wall. "I looked at it and said, *There is no way I can do this. Absolutely zero way*," Dwyer recalls. But true to the Mudder creed, participants at the top encouraged her to run and jump; someone would catch her hand and pull her over. She took her best running start, jumped, scrambled up the wall, and then hands reached out to grab her and pulled her over. "I was amazed that I did it and felt almost giddy. I loved the support and knew from that moment I would be able to do this."

Her worst obstacle was jumping into an ice pool and then repeatedly plunging under a series of barrels dispersed throughout a cold body of water. "My entire body froze and I got an intense headache rush and earache," she says. "My limbs wouldn't work when I had to climb the ladder out of the icy water. I had to get pulled out by my siblings." Despite the headache and earache, she continued on.

The next memorable obstacle was jumping off a twenty-foot wall into more water. As she climbed up the ladder, she told the marine stationed at the top that he might just have to push her in. "No problem," came the quick response. She jumped before she could think about it and went underwater. While struggling her way back up to the surface, the next jumper landed too close to her and kicked her in the head.

Through every obstacle, her family offered support and encouragement. She never opted out of an obstacle, which is allowable. They went through the Electroshock Therapy obstacle together, the crown jewel of every Tough Mudder event. The goal is to get through the live voltage wires without getting shocked, but that's impossible. Everyone gets shocked; it's just a matter of how much. In some of the electric shock obstacles, the wires hang down and the participants run through them. In others, the participants crawl through mud to avoid them. And in still others, the shocks surround a balance beam; fall off the beam and you get shocked. Brandon got shocked so many times, his arm went into violent and painful convulsions.

There were obstacles Dwyer found fun, like the monkey bars and jumping over the fire pits. But toward the end of the day, into the third hour, she was tired, cold, and starting to get miserable because she couldn't get rid of the chill. Despite all that, her spirits were high. The last obstacle involved running through more electrical shocks. They finished as a group and then the partying began. Dwyer recounts the finish: "We felt so badass! We all put on our well-earned orange headbands, the treasured medal so to speak, and rehashed the course and all the obstacles, what we liked, what we didn't like. Mom took lots of photos and then we piled into the car, still dirty and covered in mud, and went out for dinner. We were tired but excited. This family rolls with anything!"

For Eva, part of the challenge and fun of doing the TM was figuring out how to conquer each obstacle. She has a very analytical mind and uses it well. For instance, when the six of them were faced with the obstacle called Everest, a curved wall that's rounded at the top with a rush of water flowing down its slope—a keystone Tough Mudder obstacle that is all about teamwork—she made a quick analysis of who out of the six of them could get up the wall first while climbing on everyone's shoulders, then who would go next, and so on until the last person got pulled up and hauled over by everyone else.

Comparing her TM experience with running marathons, Dwyer likes that she wasn't pressured by a clock. "It's not about time. I liked the challenge and the camaraderie and sharing that with my siblings and dad. That was the only goal. I could never have done this on my own, and that's what I enjoyed the most." For her, marathons are an individual experience. "There is so much training and mental prep that goes into running 26.1 miles. Four to five months of your life goes into the training. I would never do a marathon on a lark or without training, like I did for the TM." Marathons are definitely harder!

Dwyer says that the TM didn't change her in any way, but she is glad she experienced it. She adds that she didn't have any goals going in and wasn't looking for a life-changing event.

She feels that Tough Mudders appeal to a wide audience such as the high-energy social person looking for a challenge that doesn't take over their life, and also the person who likes to help others succeed— like the guy on top of the wall who got a thrill from helping people over.

Dave Dwyer, fifty-seven, the patriarch of the family, rarely says no to an event that includes his kids. He and his wife, Joan, married young, nineteen and twenty respectively, and in some ways are just like kids to their kids. They taught the children to be independent and loyal to one another. When Dwyer ran the 2013 New York City Marathon with his daughter Robin, he described it as a fantastic experience, running together side by side the entire way. He felt she could have run faster and at mile 20 encouraged her to go for it and get a faster time. In the last few miles, she pulled ahead but kept looking back. Finally, she said: "Dad, this is no time to slow down, come on!" They crossed the finish line together.

For his first Tough Mudder, he added strength training and weight resistance to his usual running routine, but nothing too specific; he felt that the TM wasn't going to be as physically challenging as his marathons or the Hood to Coast Relay. There were some challenging elements—ice-water plunges, electric shocks, an eighteen-foot-high jump into water—but nothing that was that taxing from a fitness standpoint. For Dave, the event was all about being with his family.

"It was a blast doing this with my kids," he says. "They approached it as a team event and were there to have fun and be very supportive of one another. We laughed a lot and had a good time."

He makes a point of not completely minimizing the intensity of the event. They were all challenged, and at the end of the day felt proud of themselves for having finished. And that includes his wife, Joan, whom he gives major kudos to for always supporting their craziness and being the first to say go for it. "I think she is the most competitive of the group," he laughs.

Eva Rose hasn't done another obstacle course race, but her sister Amelia, who lives in Colorado, has. Like Eva, she has been athletic her whole life and was on board from the get-go. "As a family we are insanely competitive so doing the event with my sisters and dad looked like a fun challenge," says Amelia. Like Eva, she didn't train but was in shape from running a couple of days a week, snowboarding, and white-water rafting. And like Eva, she is not a quitter. A few times on the course she wanted to rest or eat something, but she never quit. Since completing her first OCR, she has entered a few more. "I love the challenge," says Amelia. "It feels great to finish them, another notch on the belt. Each time I have found a great group of friends to do them with and it is a whole weekend event." What keeps her coming back is also the feeling of accomplishment, team bonding, athletic skill, and sheer adventure.

The Tough Mudder taught Amelia that she is an adrenaline junkie: "Being outside, getting challenged, wet, dirty, a little crazy: That's what I look for in an event now. I need the adrenaline!"

The Dwyer family fits the profile of OCR competitors. They want to be challenged, don't mind getting dirty, love the camaraderie and one another—and at the end of the day it's all about the badass photos.

ALYSSA FERRARO

26, Ridgewood New Jersey

"Always an athlete."

Since age six, Alyssa Ferraro has been a competitor. Four hours a day, five days a week, she practiced her gymnastics and on weekends traveled with a club team throughout the tristate area (New York, New Jersey, and Connecticut). She loved the camaraderie of the other girls, referring to them as her sisters. And they were good, competing at the national level. For twelve years, her life consisted of *practice, compete, rest, repeat.* "I loved it," she says. "It fit my personality, as I like to be busy and am very goal-oriented. I get antsy if I don't do something every day." Statuesque and stunning, with long dark hair flowing over her shoulders, Ferraro exudes a composed grace. It's hard to imagine her covered in mud and liking it.

In college, she switched sports to diving and competed all four years on the University of Pittsburgh diving team. It was a new challenge for her, and she enjoyed the learning process. "I went from landing on my feet to landing on my head," she laughs. Her parents made the drive from New Jersey to Pittsburgh to watch her compete. After graduating in 2010, she moved back to New Jersey and landed a job with Genesco Sports Enterprises, a sports marketing agency, a perfect fit given her love of sports.

But as most post-collegiate athletes soon find, it's not easy to keep up with your chosen sport, especially one like diving. "I got a little paranoid after college about not being on a team or having a sport to do," she recalls. "For the first time since age six I wasn't on a team. I was on my own." Her mother, a runner, encouraged her to take up running, and soon she was entering races. "I took to it well and really liked the discipline and workouts," says Ferraro.

Still, she found running a bit lonely. She states: "It's just me and my thoughts out there. I found running mentally challenging." She started looking around for something else to do, something different and fun, and found a Spartan Sprint.

In 2011, OCRs were still relatively new. Ferraro signed up for a Spartan Sprint in June with three girlfriends. "I didn't know what to expect but I thought it would be fun," she says. "Something different that incorporated running and upper-body strength, which I was in shape for. Plus, I was intrigued to roll around in the mud as part of an event."

Her team consisted of a former cheerleader and gymnast, her former gymnastics coach—who was forty at the time—and another gymnastics coach that Ferraro worked with, as she was coaching gymnastics part-time. "We all shared the same strong work ethic, and were in shape to pull this off," she says. They went online to study the course and the obstacles but none of them felt they needed to train. Their goal was just to have fun.

The event took place in Tuxedo, New York, a short drive for them. They followed some of the online tips such as avoiding baggy shorts. They wore spandex Dri-Fit shorts and bright yellow tops. The color was selected as they thought it would stand out even when covered in mud. They registered as individuals, not as a team, realizing that their competitive drive would take over sooner or later.

Driving up that morning, the feeling in the car was, *Holy shit, why are we doing this?* When they arrived, more than a thousand participants were milling around waiting for the start. The four-mile course was on a ski slope. As Ferraro was waiting for her wave to start at the bottom of the hill, she looked up and thought, *What was I thinking!* The first obstacle was reaching the top of the slope. She and everyone else took off, running straight up. Within minutes, almost everyone was walking. Ferraro was determined not to walk, though toward the top she had to do some walk-running. Still, she did run most of it. "It was really steep," she recalls.

The women started out together as a group, but the super-competitive one took off while two fell behind. Ferraro was in the middle and did a quick analysis to determine if she wanted to wait for the others or continue on her own. She slowed a bit and the two others caught up with her. At the top of the hill, they gave her permission to go on without them.

The second obstacle was a series of beams that she had to jump over, then crawl under, at all different heights. It was very doable and she was having a lot of fun. At that point she was ready for more challenging obstacles, and soon found them. Next she had to fill a bucket with rocks and carry it a quarter mile up the hill, then back down. The buckets were hard to carry, with skinny handles. Some participants tried to carry them on their shoulders, but that left bruises. "I thought I'd never make it to the top," she says. In another one, she had to crawl a quarter mile uphill through a river of cold mud filled with rocks and sticks, canopied by barbed wire. At that point she was getting tired, the mud was cold, and to make matters worse her hair got caught in the barbed wire. But she persevered, and maintained a sense of humor. "Crawling though mud with barbed wire over my head isn't something I ever expected to do but it sort of gave me a thrill," she says. "I was still having fun, but hoping it would end soon."

Through it all, she never wanted to quit, never backed away from an obstacle, and did them all alone. The final obstacle was actually the finish-line chute, but it was lined with Spartan volunteers holding rubber jousting bats aiming to knock down everyone trying to get to the finish. She definitely got nervous at that one, but managed to dodge most of the blows and finally finished. Her first thought was, *Wow! That was fun.*

Her time was just over an hour, which placed her in the top percent of finishers. One month later she signed up for another OCR, a Rugged Maniac. "I really enjoyed my first OCR so was on board when the same girls and others asked me to join them," she states. Because she was still running and coaching gymnastics, and did so well at the Spartan event, she didn't do any training for it. On their website, Rugged Maniacs are described as "a day filled with 25 epic obstacles, a crazy party, and plenty of beer. Run our 3-mile course where you'll climb towers of shipping containers, rocket down a 50' waterslide, bounce on trampolines, jump over fire, and more!" She didn't find it as challenging as the Spartan course but had fun doing it. And because some of her teammates were not in shape and had never done an OCR, they stuck together as a team, helping one another. "As much as I like to do these on my own and test myself, I really enjoyed the team camaraderie and helping others achieve their goal. It was very inspiring to see my friends who didn't think they could do it dig down and finish. We all celebrated their accomplishments at the end," she adds. "That was rewarding for me."

A year later, in July 2012, she signed up for a Warrior Dash in Englishtown, New Jersey. By now she knew what to expect from them and added strength training to her running and gymnastics. She also decided to run her first half-marathon that September, so her running advanced to a more rigorous training schedule. But this is what Ferraro thrives on: being busy, being athletic, and enjoying the competition. She also found out she likes rolling around in mud.

In terms of difficulty, she places the Warrior Dash between the Spartan Sprint and the Rugged Maniac. She still had fun, which, in the end, is why she does them. Comparing them to her first half-marathon experience later that year, she says: "The half-marathon was definitely more of a mental challenge and more of a serious goal for me. In the Spartan Sprint, which was my most difficult OCR, I used muscles all over my body and in the end I was more exhausted. But I have to say that I felt more proud of myself when I finished my half-marathon."

Ferraro hasn't done any more OCRs, but she ran the 2014 Chicago Marathon, her first, and loved it. The months of training, the coaching, and the workouts were familiar to her and appealed to her rigorous work ethic. "I've been an athlete all my life and I feel that the effort I put into the marathon was much more than what I did for my OCRs."

For Ferraro, OCRs are just for fun, something to do with a group of friends, a day spent in the mud. She says it's much easier to get a group of friends together to do a Warrior Dash, say, than to go out and run a 5K race. "It's more enticing to the non-runners to do an OCR," she explains. "Not many non-runners get excited to run three miles, but tell them they'll be crawling through mud and jumping over fire pits and they say, 'I'm there!'"

Adding obstacle course racing to her résumé didn't change Ferraro.

"I've been an athlete my entire life and already had a strong work ethic to begin with," she summarizes. "My athletic background certainly helped get me through some of the more challenging obstacles, but I enjoy them more for the fun and social aspect of doing this with my girlfriends."

Ferraro is getting married in the fall of 2015. Her fiancé, Ben, enjoys sports as much as she does. There's an old saying that if you really want to know someone, travel with them. Ferraro has already traveled with Ben, so she notched that up a bit and invited him to do some OCRs with her. To her delight, he likes getting muddy as much as she does. Sounds like a match made in heaven.

KATHERINE "KC" FRAHM

29, Rolla, Missouri

"Finding myself."

Nothing in KC Frahm's life would point to her future as a passionate obstacle course race participant. Looking back on her former obese self, she doesn't even recognize that person. Nowadays the radio personality from Missouri spends most of her weekends participating in OCRs.

Frahm was born and raised on a small farm out in the country. Both of her parents were public schoolteachers. Her dad was also a football and track coach. "I think he always dreamed of his daughter being the shining athlete, but I have been overweight since second grade and was much more of a band nerd than any type of athlete," says KC. "He never said he was disappointed in me, but often gave me a hard time about my eating choices and lifestyle habits as I was growing up." She looks back on her eating habits on the farm and points to portion control—too much food on the plate—and a diet heavy on meat and potatoes as contributing to her weight. Plus not being active, a bit of a couch potato.

Her successful trumpet playing in high school earned her a full scholarship to attend college in Hawaii. Feeling somewhat sheltered after her farm days, she wanted to go to college as far away as possible—and she got her wish. She cherished her time in Hawaii but regretted that she wasn't in the physical condition that would allow her to do many of the outdoor activities she would have liked. At 275 pounds, she couldn't complete many hikes such as the beautiful and iconic Stairway to Heaven Hike on Oahu, with its great vistas.

After college she returned to Missouri in 2010 and faced a troubled economy and job market. To get by, she volunteered for National Public Radio and did clerical work at a local hospital. She missed Hawaii and dreamed about traveling to different places, resigned to being an armchair traveler. All that changed in June 2012 when a co-worker at the hospital put out a post on Facebook saying she would be traveling to Vermont for an event called the "Spartan Death Race" and was looking for support crew; she would pay for all expenses on the trip if some-one would just go along. Frahm jumped at the chance at a free trip to New England. "I honestly had no idea what a Death Race was or how much it would impact my life at the time," she recalls. "All I knew is that I was on my way to Vermont."

Once she arrived in Pittsfield, Vermont, it didn't take KC long to recognize the caliber of the athletes attending the event. The Spartan Death Race, with the tagline "You may Die," was created in 2004 by Joe DeSena and Andy Weinberg, who went on to create the Spartan Series OCRs. It lasts for up to seventy hours, and no one sleeps. Not even the crew. "I was on call twenty-four seven to assist my friend with whatever she needed," says Frahm, "like food, water, or just moral sup-port." She tried to accompany her friend up a mountain but had to stop midway. "I was close to 300 pounds and in no shape to be doing that type of physical activity. I was mortified. Here were these athletes traversing the mountain twenty times over the course of three days and I couldn't even do it once," says Frahm.

Over her weekend in Vermont, Frahm learned a lot about the human ability to achieve great things and overcome obstacles, both physical and mental, and also learned a few things about herself. She recalls: "I did a lot of thinking once I got back to Missouri about where I was health-wise and where I wanted to be. I also wanted to learn more about obstacle course racing and how I could do one." She was attracted to the communal spirit of the OCR community and how everyone gave support to one another. She also liked the idea of working with a team and being part of the one-for-all-and-all-for-one mentality. "I wanted a change, and this was my opening."

She had always been pretty good at losing weight but not keeping it off, losing and gaining the same seventy-five or so pounds. She looked into bariatric surgery and decided it would be a good choice for her, as her nemesis was portion control. If she could cut down on her portions—something the surgery helps with—she felt she could do the rest through her own willpower and determination. To prepare, she lost sixty pounds prior to her surgery and then seventy more afterward. She doesn't always mention to people that she had surgery, not because she is ashamed of it but because there is such a stigma to it. Some people feel it's the easy way out or a quick fix to weight loss. "I don't feel like I took the easy way out," she says. "I still have to be careful what I eat and exercise on a regular basis."

Once her weight started to drop, the next step was to get in shape. She went from walking to running, then trained to run 5Ks. She was feeling good about herself and managed to keep the weight off. Then she upped her game—drastically. In March 2014 she took a big leap and signed up for the Bataan Memorial Death March, a challenging marathon through the high desert terrain of the White Sands Missile Range in New Mexico, conducted in honor of the heroic service members who defended the Philippine Islands during World War II. Everyone told her she was crazy. What prompted her to go from zero to one hundred in a single bound? "Why not?" she laughs. "I wanted something so insurmountable that to achieve it would prove I was capable of anything."

She worked with a personal trainer, took CrossFit classes, and every weekend for months went on long walk/runs. She was one of fewer than one hundred women to complete the event, carrying over forty pounds on her back the entire time. "So many people in my life said there was no way I could possibly finish that, but that drove me even more to succeed," she states with pride. It took her nine hours to finish the march. What she learned from the experience is that anything is possible, and that she could set her sights as high as she wanted.

After the Bataan March she decided to concentrate on OCRs as a way to stay fit and enjoy the camaraderie of like-minded folks. Her first OCR was in July 2014, a local event called the Fugitive Race: four miles and a hundred obstacles. She didn't train, as it was just four months after her Bataan event. However, she did keep up with her personal training sessions and worked on her upper-body strength, hitting the gym three to five times a week. Six months later she took another big leap, completing a Spartan Sprint and a Super event back-to-back during a weekend in Chicago. For that event she added trail running to her training to build her ankle strength, hoping to avoid injuries on the rocky trails.

The double Spartan was challenging and very hilly. She was grateful for the training she put in and thrilled that she didn't come in last, but realized she needed to do more training and get in even better shape if she was going to continue to participate in OCRs in a more serious fashion. Her worst obstacle in the event was the Box Jump. When she was training for this obstacle she fell, hit her head on concrete, and got a concussion. When she faced that obstacle in the event, she felt fear growing in her stomach at the memory of the fall and had to suck it up to overcome it. As Frahm came to realize, part of doing OCRs is learning to overcome fears.

Another obstacle that's always been her nemesis is the Spartan Slippery Wall, a slanted near-vertical wall. Not only is it slick, but participants have to go through water before climbing it so it's wet as well. There are ropes to help on the climb, but with her upper body being weak, she always struggled getting over the wall and needed assistance, a firm push from behind. In her February 2015 Spartan Sprint, though, she finally conquered the obstacle. "I kept thinking to myself, *I can see the finish line from here, just do it!*" And with that shot of adrenaline and determination, she was finally able to get herself up and over the wall. "It was an incredible feeling of accomplishment."

In October 2014 Frahm completed the Spartan Beast in Dallas, Texas, a milestone. "My medal is now complete," she says, referring to the Spartan Challenge in which racers complete three distances—a Sprint, a Super, and the Beast—in a single year. The three medal pieces interlock together to form the Trifecta medal.

That's quite a string of endurance racing in less than eight months. "I'm very goal-oriented," says Frahm. "My long-term goal was to do thirty OCRs by the time I turn thirty in May 2016, but I've already completed those so I guess I need a new goal." And that was accomplished along with juggling two jobs, as the radio program director and host of NPR's *All Things Considered* for KMST, Missouri.

What motivates Frahm to take on such extreme challenges? Some of the reasons stem from her life when she was obese. She can still see the obese woman inside her who needs to be quelled at times. "I started doing the extreme events to show the naysayers that I can do this," she explains. "I do a quiet little *I told you I could do this!* inside my head."

She also truly loves her OCR family, carpooling to events, sharing rooms, and supporting one another. Being in the Midwest adds a challenge because most of the events are on the East or West Coast, so carpooling is a necessity. And as a big thank-you from the organizers at Spartan who loved her weight loss story and her relentless, positive attitude and love of all things Spartan, they gifted her a year of free entries. Says Frahm: "Once I found out Spartan was gracious enough to give me the season pass, I decided to take full advantage of it. Traveling to races isn't cheap, so if I was going to travel to them I was going to push myself as hard as I could."

She keeps her medals on a rack at her home under a sign that reads, A JOURNEY OF A THOUSAND MILES STARTS WITH A SINGLE STEP, attributed to the Chinese philosopher Lao-tzu. "Spartan races changed my life," states Frahm. "I was always the geeky band kid, but look at me now. Wow! I don't think of myself as amazing, more like a work in progress. My self-confidence is growing but has a way to go. Sometimes I can't believe how far I've come, but when I look back on my races and what I have achieved I realize there is no limit to what I can do."

In August 2015 Frahm has a bold event on her schedule, circled in red: the Spartan Ultra Beast, in Hawaii. As their website states, "The Ultra Beast is an exorcism." It covers more than twenty-six miles with fifty-plus obstacles and a few twists thrown in to keep it interesting. No map or details for the course are available, so participants don't have a clue what they are getting into. "A lot of my Hawaii friends and 'family' have not seen me since I graduated, so if I can raise enough money to get to Hawaii that's something I very much want to do this year," says a hopeful Frahm on her trip (still pending at the time of this writing).

Frahm has become something of a local Spartan ambassador. She loves to give back to the Spartan community for all they have given her. She encourages new recruits and stays with them during their first event, providing motivation, cheers, and encouragement. "It's so rewarding to watch someone finish his or her first OCR," she says. "It's a day they will never forget." And in turn, her students will surely not forget the woman with the soulful green eyes and wide smile who helped make it happen.

JERRY FUENTES

41, Baldwin, New York

"I love crazy!"

Growing up in the Bronx, Jerry Fuentes was always doing something crazy, like jumping from rooftop to rooftop, leaping off bridges, riding his bike at top speed and then jumping ramps that he set on fire to make it even riskier, riding his bike down guardrails—anything out of the ordinary. "If I was given a dare, I did it. Never even thought about what I was doing or the risks involved," recalls Fuentes. He never stayed indoors watching TV or being bored. Now a police officer for thirteen years, he knows his limits but can still do crazy.

His journey to becoming a police officer started in his Bronx high school, one of the toughest in his neighborhood. "You had to watch your back at my school. We were the first school that introduced the use of metal detectors," he says. To survive, he learned early on to become friends with all the groups—the gangs, the nerds, and the geeks. He put those skills to use and stayed out of trouble. School safety became a rallying point for him when he considered his career. He started out as a school safety officer prior to becoming a transit officer.

Fuentes has struggled with weight issues for most of his life. He ate a lot of junk food and consumed too much sugary soda. By the time he was an adult, he weighed 240 pounds (he's five foot nine) and he "felt like an old man." And his job does not require yearly physicals so he had no motivation to lose the weight. That all changed in 2011 when he received a dare from his brother-in-law.

His brother-in-law, Claudio, showed him a YouTube clip of a Spartan Sprint and asked if he wanted to do one with him. "He had me at the video," laughs Fuentes. "It looked like a lot of crazy fun, and that appealed to me. I was in from the get-go." The race was in six months. He knew he had to train and this was the motivation he needed to get in shape. He started going to the gym and walking on the treadmill. His weight prevented him from doing too much without risking injury, so he concentrated on low-impact forms of exercise like the elliptical machine.

His other motivation for getting in shape was his daughter. At the time he decided to do the Spartan Sprint, she was a toddler and just starting to be mobile. "I wanted to set a good example early on for her on how to live a healthy lifestyle," he recalls. "I wanted to run around and play with her and I knew my weight issues would get in the way of that."

The first thing he did was cut out the soda and junk food. He slowly increased his weight training sessions and added running to his routine. In six months he lost forty pounds and felt like a new man, ready to tackle his first obstacle course race. "I couldn't wait to get that medal to prove I could do it," he says. "I was so ready."

The morning of the event, he drove to Tuxedo, New York, with Claudio and another brother-in-law. He was nervous. "My biggest concern is that I didn't look like a fool in front of my family. I wasn't sure I could keep up," he states. "When I looked up at the first hill I said to myself, *Oh man, that looks like a killer*." The first wave of elites were just finishing, walking around muddy wearing their medals. That was all the motivation Fuentes needed. He said a prayer and off he went to earn that medal.

After the kickoff group cheer of "A-rooo!" the smoke bombs went off, and he started running up the hill repeating his mantra, "This too shall end." After fifty yards, he was sucking air and had to walk. With the help of spectators cheering for him and his buddies encouraging him to keep moving forward, he finally made it to the top of the mountain. "I was tired and sore and full of scratches but at no point did I want to quit. I was excited to be there."

Seeing all kinds of body types, some in better shape but some not, inspired him as well and gave him confidence. One of his toughest obstacles was the uphill mud crawl. Within seconds, he realized this wasn't just mud. It was mud laced with gravel and stones, with barbed wire on top. "This was real barbed wire, not fake stuff," he laughs. "Everywhere I placed my hands, there was something underneath the mud with sharp edges. I got into a barrel roll to move forward, but with every roll I lost ground and rolled backward. And you can't stand up because of the barbed wire."

At that point he was thankful for the hours he'd put in at the gym, because he needed to rely on his core strength to get through the mud. The obstacles got progressively worse, but with the support of his buddies he kept going. When faced with the rope climb, though, he balked. In this obstacle, he had to crawl into a muddy water pit, climb a twenty-five-foot rope, and ring the bell at the top. By the time he got to the rope, he was covered in what felt like an extra fifteen pounds of mud. He got halfway up the rope and gave up, falling back into the muddy water. He knew this would be his nemesis, and instead of wasting more energy he did his thirty Burpees and moved on.

(The Burpee is a common feature of OCR courses and training. You squat, then thrust your feet out rearward and assume the "plank" position, then pull your feet back in, and finally stand back up. And repeat.)

As he plowed his way through the obstacle course, he wondered if he would finish in one piece. "I was tested to the limit," he recalls. "I was tired, cold, covered in mud, and zapped of all energy." But he did make it to the finish and with a yell and a whoop proudly put on his finisher's medal. "I couldn't wait to do another one," he boldly states. "That medal is my most prized possession."

The entire family celebrated that night. He felt he had achieved greatness. He was also proud to share the moment with his wife and daughter and show them anything is possible. Three days later he signed up for his next OCR.

But the next one wasn't for another year and he was dying to stay shape and motivated, so in September he signed up for the 9/11 Memorial Bike Ride, 360 miles from New York City to the Pentagon. It was the first anniversary of 9/11. Fuentes was one of eight hundred police officers who took part. By the end of the ride he was in the best shape of his life, down to 180 lean and mean pounds. He set a new goal to lose 10 more and get to 170.

One year after his first Spartan Sprint, Fuentes did another Spartan Sprint followed by a Spartan Super two months later. He got so hooked on OCRs that he convinced friends, family members, and other police officers to join him. He formed a team called The Usual Suspects and became the trainer and head cheerleader. His first team had forty-five members with a core group of twenty. He gives them a training program that includes some cardio and weight training as well as motivational tips—*Never quit*; *Keep moving*. Since he formed The Usual

Suspects, no one has ever quit a course. "They may hate it, they may get cursed at to keep moving, but they all finish and love it in the end," says Fuentes.

In 2013 he completed another Spartan Sprint and Super and added his first triathlon to his growing list of athletic achievements. He watched a YouTube video on learning to swim. When he got the confidence to jump into a pool and try out his technique, he was spent after two laps. Not one to give up, he asked other swimmers at the pool for tips and techniques. He also practiced with a new mantra: "It's only one day!"

For Fuentes, 2014 went down as his "Year of the Races." He completed five Spartan races, including his first Spartan Beast; the New York City Olympic distance triathlon; and a few 5Ks. He was basically either training or going to events every weekend until his wife said *enough!* He agreed and was ready for a break after achieving his biggest goal, the Spartan Trifecta, which culminates with the Beast. That event took place in Killington, Vermont, and took him eight and a half hours to complete. His wife came along for moral support.

At the time of this writing, his race agenda includes a BattleFrog event, a half Ironman, a century (one-hundred-mile) bike ride, and completing another Trifecta. He manages to do all the training and events and still put his family first. "My wife thinks I am going through a midlife crisis, but this is my life now. I love the challenge and pushing myself to new limits. This is a whole new world for me and I love it," he says. Despite her worries and concerns, his wife is his biggest supporter and he needs her in his corner. They have a strong marriage and help each other attain their individual and combined goals.

Fuentes is a changed man. Since training for his first Spartan Sprint in 2011, he is now down to 170 pounds from 240 and never felt better. "Spartan races got me off the couch and into the best shape of my life," says Fuentes. "And I'm more confident on the job because of my new-found strength and physique. I also spend hours playing with my daughter and teaching her about the importance of exercise in her life."

Because he took a dare, a whole new world opened up for Fuentes. Now he can't imagine his life without OCRs.

JOE GALLITANO

34, Brooklyn, New York

"Travel to faraway lands. Meet interesting people.
Eat their food. Run it off later."

Joe Gallitano has many interests. When not spending his time in the financial markets, he maintains a rigorous training schedule, and is constantly visiting farmers markets and cooking up what he finds. His wanderlust has taken him on some interesting journeys, many motivated by races or food. He spends a lot of time talking about and thinking about food, everything from green smoothies to duck egg bacon burgers to Bailey's French toast. He needs a fairly large intake of calories because he is constantly either training for a race or competing in one. And he is very competitive. He has been running as long as he can remember, from setting up races with friends in kindergarten to high school track meets to more recent ultramarathons.

Gallitano grew up in Elk Grove, Illinois. He crewed at the University of Michigan, where his team placed in the top ten nationally. "I learned a lot about hard work, determination, and digging deep while I rowed," says Gallitano. After graduating in 2004, he needed a new goal and took up running. He ran the 2006 Chicago Marathon, finishing in 4:06, respectable for a first-timer—but not for him. He trained harder, read about nutrition and anything else that would make him a better runner, and in time improved his marathon finish to a 3:42. In 2009, there was buzz about a Warrior Dash OCR coming to Chicago (Joliet), and he immediately signed up with a group of friends. "The unknown appealed to me," recalls Gallitano. "I'd never done one and it seemed doable. As an added bonus, we learned how to throw axes."

As a marathoner, he knew the three-mile course wouldn't be a problem, and he had the endurance and upper-body strength from his rowing background. His first OCR was done to test the waters and see if it was something he could take on in a more serious way. He and his friends had a blast and immediately signed up for another one. "We had a ton of fun and you get a free beer at the end."

He entered the same event in 2010, and his team did even better. Gallitano was starting to think that OCRs could be what he'd been looking for since leaving college. He continued running marathons, but in May 2012 he signed up for his first Tough Mudder and qualified for the World's Toughest Mudder—in Englishtown, New Jersey, the following December. That event has gone down in Tough Mudder history as epic for its weather—so cold that more than half the participants came down with hypothermia, Gallitano included. It wasn't so much the degree of cold that did him in as it was his wet suit—which ripped and allowed cold water to come streaming in. He ended up with uncontrollable shakes and had to drop out. "It was a horrible experience," he recalls. "I trained really hard and think I could have done well but it's those unexpected conditions that get you."

Not a quitter, Gallitano trained like a demon all throughout 2013 for the next World's Toughest Mudder. He dedicated more time to his training, worked out harder at the gym, and the Saturday before the event ran thirty miles to make sure he was ready. This time he stayed on the course throughout the full twenty-four hours, hitting his goal of running fifty miles. "That race threw everything at me but I was determined to finish," says Gallitano. He had some tough moments, like crawling through a sewage tube in the middle of the night and getting claustrophobic. "It's extremely primal, crawling exhausted through mud and rocks when you can barely see anything around you." When he finished, the sense of accomplishment was overwhelming. "I survived!" he exclaims.

Feeling empowered, he signed up for the 2014 Spartan Death Race in Pittsfield, Vermont, as the ultimate test of endurance and mental toughness. Competitors must complete numerous grueling mental and physical challenges throughout a forty-mile (or more) course through the Vermont woods. Obstacles can include chopping wood for two hours; completing a thirty-mile hike with rocks and weighted packs; building a fire from scratch; or, after twenty-four hours of racing, memorizing the names of the first ten US presidents, then hiking to the top of a mountain and reciting them back in order. If you miss one, you do it again till you get it right. Most participants don't finish. Gallitano was feeling good until he got lost—there is no course map—and missed a cutoff time. "That was a heartbreaker for me," he says. "I really felt like I could have done it but things didn't go my way that day." Nor did they do so during the 2014 World's Toughest Mudder, his third. The morning of the start, he came down with food poisoning. Twenty-five miles into the race he almost had to call it quits, but several friends were able to walk him back to the pit, where he cleared his system, held down some food, and reentered the course. After fifty miles and twenty-four hours, he finished his second World's Toughest Mudder.

Gallitano is an interesting study. He is drawn to OCRs for the competition but also to feel a connectedness to the earth and—for lack of a better description—to his inner caveman. "I was never a Boy Scout and now I have to pay to play in the woods and roll around in dirt," he laughs. "I love to run, I love a physical challenge, I love being in the elements and feeling free. OCRs have filled that gap that was missing from my life."

In his job raising capital and developing client relationships for private market firms, he has to travel a lot and has developed his own training schedule. He does a lot of yoga and Pilates, spends a lot of time in hotel gyms, and travels with a GoRuck bag at all times. "For me, doing OCRs is my way of connecting with friends, blowing off steam, and challenging myself. It's also a good way to stay in shape," says Gallitano. "It's certainly different than my day job!"

In February 2015, he kicked off the year with a race in Nicaragua, the Fuego y Agua Survival Run. Along with ascents and descents of a volcano or two, participants are challenged with climbing, swimming lakes and jungle rivers, carrying all sorts of things, digging, running brutal terrain, throwing (maybe throwing up), memorizing, and just plain surviving this epic event. The obstacles are not revealed until race day. It was his hardest and favorite race ever. He followed that up in April with a Spartan Beast and in May with The North Face fifty-miler in New York.

Gallitano is a true ambassador for OCRs with a lot of passion for the sport. He loves helping newcomers get comfortable. "It's a great community," he says. "OCRs are fun, rewarding, and you meet great people. We're all a bit quirky." If Gallitano had his way, everyone would experience at least one OCR in their life and be that Boy or Girl Scout for a day. "We are all capable of much more than we know. It's a great way to find that out."

CHAUNCEY HOFFMANN

37, Chicago Illinois

"That was weird!"

Chauncey Hoffmann knows what it's like to be tough and to dig deep. She started rowing at age fourteen and has been competitively rowing and instructing since then, competing in regattas from the Midwest to the East Coast. She has run six marathons and is a CrossFit fanatic. She's also a talented architect with a great sense of humor. You'd think she would be the perfect candidate for an obstacle course race, but here's her secret . . . she doesn't like to get muddy. That's one reason she describes her first OCR as the weirdest thing she has ever done.

Hoffmann has always followed her own path in life. As an architect, her specialty is affordable multifamily housing projects. She likes to keep her designs ecofriendly. She coaches crew at the Chicago Rowing Union (CRU), a lesbian, gay, bisexual, and transgender (LGBT) rowing organization, one of only a few such clubs in the world. This is a woman who takes risks, puts herself out there, and follows her beliefs. She'd heard of OCRs and had a few friends who'd tried them, but she wasn't interested. As she explains, "I don't like getting muddy and when you look at the photos on the websites, everyone is covered in mud. Not doing that!" And registration can be expensive, more so than marathons. But when one of the coaches at her club suggested they form a team—and that he had a Groupon for the event that brought the cost down to $50 per person—she decided to give it a try.

The team chose a Spartan Sprint, which seemed the least muddy of all the OCRs. At least that's what Hoffmann thought when she compared a Tough Mudder—the word *mud* was in the name, so it was eliminated—with a Spartan event. "I was hoping to get through the course without being submerged in mud, but I was," she laughs. If she had read the course description that was posted on the site—"on a dry day the course is very muddy, and if it rains, even walking becomes difficult"—she probably wouldn't have done it. And the other major reason for picking Spartan over Tough Mudder was to avoid the Electroshock Therapy obstacle. "No way I was doing that," states Hoffmann.

Her team consisted of nine members, seven men and one other

woman, all of varying skills and strengths. Some were competitive and some not. One was an out-of-shape smoker. The team quickly realized that they had two factions: One wanted to compete and stay ahead, and the other, Hoffmann's group, just wanted to experience the event and have fun. They signed up a month before the September 2014 event in Chicago. Hoffmann didn't do any extra training for it beyond her CrossFit and rowing. She knew she was fit enough to get through the three miles and ten obstacles, as her CrossFit routine includes rope climbing, Burpees, and scampering over cargo nets. But when they arrived that morning and she got a look at some of the obstacles, she got scared. Real scared. When everyone started to do the Spartan chant at the start, she came up with her own—"Oh no, why am I here?"

The first obstacle came even before the starting line. It was an eight-foot wall that she had to get over. "There was no way I was getting over that freaking wall by myself," she recalls. "So I was pushed and pulled over." This was not a good start. The walls would become her nemesis.

Despite being pushed and prodded over most of the walls, she was able to do many of the obstacles on her own thanks to her training. She found the Atlas Balls—carrying seventy-pound balls of cement—challenging but doable, and completed that obstacle without assistance. "Anything that didn't involve getting pushed and pulled was a treat for me!"

She enjoyed being with the team and helping the other members. Even the competitive faction stayed at the harder obstacles to help out and cheer on their teammates. "We had a lot of fun because we didn't take ourselves seriously," says Hoffmann.

As she made her way through the course, she started to get tired. The three-mile trail went through lots of woods, so she could never see what was up ahead. "Every twist and turn of the course was a surprise," she laughs. "Some were good surprises like when I could actually do the obstacle on my own, but others weren't and I knew I'd have to get pushed and pulled over a wall again." She liked her teammates, but one turned out to be a grump, which affected the team dynamics. "He hated every minute of being on the course. I don't even know why he came," says Hoffmann. "He was a big guy and always needed help getting through the obstacles. By the time we hoisted him over the last wall, we all celebrated and he actually smiled for the first time all day."

When Hoffmann could finally see the finish, she got excited—but a series of difficult obstacles in the last half mile lay in the way of finishing. "We had to swim across a mud pit, climb ropes, go under a wall into more mud, and run through fire," she recalls. "It was like they threw the kitchen sink of obstacles at us right at the finish when we were bone-tired." Her first thought upon finishing was how cool it was that she'd done it. The grumpy guy celebrated by lighting up a cigarette.

Even though she is signed up for another with her brother and aunt, Hoffman is not going to become an OCR fanatic. She'd rather run marathons and do her CrossFit. But after completing her first OCR, she understands how people get addicted. "It's like a cult mentality," she explains. "They are fun, different, challenging, it's the hot thing right now, and the team concept is hard to beat. And it's easier than running a marathon or even a half-marathon." Hoffmann enjoys the team camaraderie in training, but when it comes to the event she would rather go solo. "I enjoy distance running because it is just me and my thoughts out there. I love the mental game, relying on myself and having that singular thought in your head that drives you to the finish." She continues: "In crew if one person is off, the whole boat suffers. On our Spartan team, that one grumpy guy brought us all down. But in running, it's just me. I'm not responsible for anyone, just myself."

Another reason she won't become an OCR junkie is the damn walls and mud. "I was pushed and pulled over walls so many times I just got sick of being hoisted over. Of course I appreciated the help, but really. Enough is enough. And there was too much mud!" Hoffmann is glad she had the experience and conquered her first OCR. "You learn a lot about yourself," she says. "It's good to try just one." As long as someone like a friend or family member sets it up, she'll go along for the fun. Just don't ask her to get too muddy.

DAVE HUCKLE

34, Los Angeles

*"We're all one big crazy family and
we love helping each other."*

Dave Huckle is a self-described OCR addict. In 2013 he set the
record for the most Spartan Race Trifectas in one year: nine. He is also
an extremely likable guy, the kind of person you would want as a best

friend, brother, or Spartan buddy. More than thirty-five hundred members of the OCR community think he's very likable as well. That's the current number of people in the Weeple Army, the OCR community that Huckle started in 2011. All this from a mild-mannered kid with a Mohawk haircut who struggles to find enough hours in the day for his teaching job, training for his OCR events, daily posts on Facebook, Instagram, and Twitter, and creating YouTube videos like his Floating Lotus challenge. Not to mention his car, the Weeple Wagon.

Huckle was born in Australia, the son of a navy man. He and his family were stationed at different bases around the globe during his school years, never staying in one place long enough for him to join a sports team. He attended the College of William and Mary in Virginia, the first place he'd stayed put in for more than three years, graduating in 2002. He majored in computer science, worked for the football team, and took snowboarding classes with bus trips to Maine. On his second trip, he broke his arm. But he was not to be dissuaded, a character trait that would serve him well later in life.

After graduation he took a job as a snowboarding instructor in the Appalachian Mountains of North Carolina. He loved his job, and with his good-natured and easygoing personality, he made a lot of friends—including his future wife, Heather, who met Dave when she took a lesson from him. They moved to Florida in 2005. "I felt so lucky," says Huckle. "Everything was falling into place. Now I just needed a real job." He got hired teaching science to middle school kids and was a natural. The kids loved him and his engaging style.

In 2007 Heather, an actress, moved to Los Angeles for her career, and they endured a bicoastal engagement/marriage for a year and a half as he finished earning his teaching credential before joining her on the West Coast. He has spent the last seven years teaching middle school math in a Title 1 school where the entire student population is eligible for the National School Lunch Program. "Some of these kids have it really rough," he comments. "When I see students embrace learning and change their whole attitude about academics, I know I am making a difference in their lives."

Some of his students were part of Students Run LA (SRLA), a program started in 1987 by high school teacher Harry Shabazian, who ran the 1986 Los Angeles Marathon and was transformed by it. He thought the training and discipline it takes to run a marathon would be good for his students, who were labeled as underachievers and forgotten by the system. The next year a handful of his students took up his challenge and finished the marathon. They were some of the first kids in the school to go on to college and get jobs. Since then, thousands of kids have taken the SRLA challenge and 99 percent complete the LA Marathon every year.

One of Huckle's students was in the program and challenged him to run the marathon with him. "This seventh grader came up to me and said, 'Mr. Huckle, why aren't you running the marathon?' I had never run more than a mile in my life, but I figured if a seventh grader can do it, so could I!"

That marathon turned Huckle, who once said he hated to run, into a runner. He and his friend Patrick O'Leary (who lived in Northern California at the time) started entering 5Ks, traveling and running a race together every month. But it was when they discovered the Down & Dirty mud run that their lives changed. "This was way more fun than running a road race," says Huckle. "It was more interesting, way more dirty, and we just laughed through it."

Where did the name *Weeple* come from? Huckle explains that it originated with the Weezer song "My Name Is Jonas," which he and O'Leary listened to a lot in high school. One line, "My name is Wakefield," was misheard by O'Leary as "My name is Weeple." They had used the name for their online gaming clan in college, so it was reborn as a two-person running team, Team Weeple.

Huckle searched the Internet for more muddy events and found the Spartan Sprint in Malibu in November 2011. He remembers his excitement at first reading about the event. "It looks awesome," he recalls saying to O'Leary. "This is too cool, it has mud, fire, and you get to crawl under barbed wire. You have to see the video on their website, it's sick!" They signed up immediately and Huckle decided to expand their team of two, Team Weeple, into a much larger group. He coined the name Weeple Army.

Wanting to share his enthusiasm for the event, Huckle started recruiting more teammates through Facebook, co-workers, and personal recruitment sessions at running stores. They ended up with about twenty-eight members on the first ever Weeple Army team at that 2011 Malibu Spartan Race and decided that wasn't enough. Spartan Race held another event only two months later, and by then the Weeple Army was the largest team in the state. More than seventy members attended that race wearing their brand-new (now iconic) black-and-green Weeple Army shirts that Huckle had made. Their numbers exploded from there.

In 2012, Spartan issued a challenge to the Spartan community asking for teams to come out in force, and offering a handsome reward for the biggest team of the year. It's no surprise to anyone who knows them that the Weeples were not just the biggest team of the year but the biggest team at three different events.

As the team grew, Huckle met and included many challenged athletes with varying disabilities. Weeple Army welcomes athletes overcoming personal challenges such as those with amputations, PTSD, cancer, spina bifida, lupus, cerebral palsy, blindness, deafness, and a variety of other challenges. They even have a Facebook group (Weeples Overcoming Challenges) where people can bond through sharing their inspiring stories and training tips, and can find the support they need to complete OCRs. Everyone is equal and considered a huge part of the team, which focuses on not just finishing races but helping others along the way, even total strangers. The Weeples believe: "Anyone can do this, and everyone should do this!" Not content to complete obstacles as they are, Weeple Army members sometimes carry heavy items with them along the course—extra sandbags, giant watercooler tanks, the Weeple Army flag—or wear masks that restrict their breathing. They are impressive and crazy.

"We are all about getting people to enjoy the sport and have fun. We are the Army of Fun," says Huckle. He likes helping random people get into racing and, of course, have fun. Those signature green-and-black Weeple shirts have become synonymous with fun. Everyone notices them. If it were up to Huckle, everyone in the world would be participating in OCRs. "What is cooler to do on a weekend," he asks, "run a 5K down a street, or on a trail with mud and obstacles? When people ask you 'What did you do this weekend?' you can say, 'Oh not much. I just crawled under barbed wire, leaped over a fire pit, and rolled in mud.' Now, that is cool." He describes doing an OCR as reverting back to childhood for the day.

But more than just having fun, Huckle likes to help people accomplish their goals and dreams. Maybe that altruism was set in place by the seventh grader who challenged him to run his first marathon in 2011. He has run the Los Angeles Marathon every year since, missing only 2013 when he flew to Virginia to run his sister's first half-marathon with her. Sometimes he ran with the students, other times to raise money for charity—like when he ran blindfolded in 2014 and 2015 to help raise funds and awareness for Blind Start of America. The Weeple Army has also raised money for local schools, animal shelters, disaster relief, and veterans' charities. In 2013 they raised over $18,000 for cancer research.

Huckle believes that anyone can finish a basic OCR course, especially if you have the support of friends, a team, or the Weeple Army behind you. If you find yourself struggling with an obstacle, no worries.

Someone will be there to push, pull, or encourage you over it, under it, or through it. "It is so empowering," says Huckle. "I see the pride of achievement light up in their eyes when they complete a hard obstacle or finish a race. That makes all the time and dedication of running such a large team worth it."

This is a very busy man. He doesn't sleep much. His wife is very supportive but even she thought he was pushing the envelope when he completed an event almost every single weekend during 2013— when he set the record for most Spartan Trifectas in one year. At least he has his summers off, but then again, that offers more time to do more events. "Twenty thirteen was a crazy year," he says in an understated way. "We were busy building the Weeple Army brand so I spent a lot of time at events and posting on social media. My weeks looked something like this: Monday, work and play volleyball in the evening. Tuesday, work, rest, help with house chores. Wednesday, work and run with my local running group. Thursday, work, then do laundry and pack for the next event. Friday, work and take a red-eye to the event. Saturday, land, get to the venue, and run. Sunday race again and take a late flight home, clean all my race gear, post the event recap on social media, kiss the wife, and do it all over again."

Now he has someone else to kiss when he gets back home, his seven-month-old daughter Hunter Cricket Huckle. Not that fatherhood will slow him down. He has his eyes set on the 2015 Spartan Death Race in Vermont along with all the other events he'll do to keep building the Weeple Army. His website (www.weeplearmy.com) is offering training plans including a local OCR boot camp geared toward first-time racers. As Huckle likes to say, "Weeple Army is like the Island of Misfit Toys. A lot of people tell me they didn't know anyone who wanted to do the same 'crazy' stuff they like to do. Then in the Weeple Army they found like-minded people, and they now have a new circle of best friends. We all come from different backgrounds and have different reasons for wanting to compete, but in the end we fit together beautifully. We aren't just a running group, we are family."

MIKE JOHNSON

32, Memphis, Tennessee

"It was really tough!"

What would make a former NFL player for the Indianapolis Colts quiver with fear? What would make this same former football player, now a resident oral surgeon who recently removed a ten-inch kitchen blade from a trauma center patient and then kept his finger in the hole, pressing against the man's heart to stop the bleeding, refer to something as grueling? According to Mike Johnson, doing his first Tough Mudder was really tough.

Johnson grew up in Boulder, Colorado, with his parents and sister.

They were always outdoors, enjoying everything Boulder has to offer: skiing, cycling, running, soccer, and football. His mom was a runner and had Mike running the famous Bolder Boulder 10K race when he was six years old. He ran track in high school, but at six foot four and 215 pounds, he gravitated to football despite his parents' objections that he could get hurt. He didn't get hurt; in fact, he was recruited to play at Kansas State University. Five years later he was drafted by the Kansas City Chiefs and made it to the last cut when unfortunately he got released. But he didn't sit for long and in 2005 was picked up by the Indianapolis Colts. He started out with the practice squad and then was sent to Europe to get some game experience but ended up getting injured and had to undergo knee surgery, followed by surgery on both ankles for bone spurs. "That was a total bummer," Johnson recalls. "That year the Colts won the Super Bowl but I was on the injured reserve list and didn't make it to the game."

Johnson's years with the NFL weren't what he'd expected. His weight went up to 315 as he was consuming twelve thousand calories a day. "We ate a full meal every two hours and in between had protein shakes," he recalls. "I hated carrying around all that weight—and I was one of the smaller linemen." Football stopped being fun and became a job of survival. Unlike his college team there was no camaraderie; no friendships were formed. "Everyone looked at you as competition for their spot," he adds. His coach, a former player who'd had hip, knee, and shoulder replacements by the time he was forty-five, took Johnson under his wing and leveled with him about the NFL. "This is a business. No one gets out alive," he told him.

After a lot of deep thought, he decided to quit the NFL and applied to dental school in Denver. He grew up fixing things, always tinkering with broken appliances and discarded items he'd find on the curb. So the idea of fixing things with his hands was a natural, plus he liked the idea of having his own practice and calling his own shots. "Everything about being a dentist appealed to me. It seemed like a natural career path."

After four years of dental school, he started his residency in Memphis, Tennessee. He splits his time between hospitals and trauma centers and is on his feet for thirty-six-hour shifts. "This is one of the most physical things I have ever done," says Johnson. "It's tough to get any exercise at all. If I ever get some spare time, I sleep!" But that all changed when his chief resident asked him to do a Tough Mudder with him.

He had seen obstacle course racing advertised on websites but never thought of doing one. About six residents agreed to form a team, but three backed out. Their event was the Tough Mudder in Nashville in May 2014. Unfortunately, the previous year a death had occurred at a Tough Mudder in West Virginia; that put some trepidation and fear into Johnson and his new bride, Megan, about going forward. The April drowning was at least the fourth death involving participants at extreme obstacle course events. Johnson was determined not to become a statistic. Megan was not happy that her husband was going to take part in an obstacle race. "Let's just say she was not excited that I was doing this, so I needed to show her I was in shape," he says.

Despite the worry and fear, Johnson was excited about his first OCR. He had been looking for something to change up his normal gym routine, and the challenge of the obstacles appealed to him. "This was not going to be boring," he adds. "I was ready to get back into shape and back into competition." And he liked the concept of a team. Working in the operating room, he came to realize the importance of a team relying on one another to achieve a goal. "I liked the fact that the Tough Mudder is all about the team. When you are dog-tired it's comforting to know that your teammates are there to help."

Johnson worked out extra hard. He went right back to his football drills, running an average of three to six miles and up to fourteen, working out in the gym with generous reps of push-ups and pull-ups, lots of weight strengthening, and whatever else he felt he needed to do to stay alive. "I worked out like a maniac so I would survive," says Johnson. His years in the NFL taught him how to dig deep and get through grueling moments of pain. He also watched videos and YouTubes of the obstacles, trying to figure out how he would approach them. One obstacle, the Mount Everest Giant Half Pike, seemed particularly challenging.

On the day of the event, Megan drove Mike and the other teammates to Nashville. Johnson describes the scene as one long mud pit. Everywhere he looked he saw mud and water pits. He wore a GoPro to capture the event. As they headed out to the first obstacle, he realized there would be a lot of downtime. "You run to the obstacle and then wait till the other wave ahead of you finishes," he recalls. "So you stand around and cheer on the participants as you wait your turn." His height and strength worked in his favor for most of the obstacles. Even Mount Everest was not as daunting when he came face-to-face with it. He had done his homework, and it paid off.

He summarizes the day as one long slough through mud and ice water. He conquered every obstacle, but some stand out as particularly tough or nasty. Being the biggest member of the team, he often had to be the bottom of the pyramid, supporting everyone else on his shoulders. "I sank into so much mud, I didn't think I'd ever wash it off," he recalls. On the plus side, he loved the thrill of some of the surprise obstacles, like the waterslide that propelled him over flames at the end and dumped him into yet more ice water. "Hitting ice water definitely takes your breath away."

As in most Tough Mudders, Electroshock Therapy was one of the last obstacles. Johnson knew it was coming and dreaded it. His teammates took the easy way out, opting to forgo it and take the penalty. He was determined to do it but got zapped. His strategy of sprinting through the zone didn't work. "I got nailed and went down hard, face-first into the mud," he recalls, wincing at the memory.

When he finished, his first thought was relief that he'd made it through alive and intact except for some scratches and bruises. He was handed a beer and shown to the communal shower area, where he tried to rinse off the multiple layers of mud. There was a donation box at the showers for the dirty clothes the participants never wanted to wear again, and Johnson donated his shoes. "I was exhausted, dog-tired," says Johnson. "Megan drove us home and I collapsed in the backseat drinking gallons of Gatorade. I never would have made it home without Megan's help."

The next morning Johnson was back at work for a thirty-six-hour shift. No rest for this Mudder. What did Johnson learn from his Tough Mudder experience? "I still got it," he proudly states. "All those years of grueling football drills and practices and my dental residency have made me mentally and physically tougher than I thought." He wants to do another and is considering one in Colorado in 2016.

The preparation for that future event has already started. Johnson has stayed in shape since his 2014 event. That's the second thing he learned from his experience: "I enjoyed getting in the best shape since my NFL days," he says. "I do better with a fitness routine. It helps me stay focused."

Johnson's future looks promising. He loves what he does and is constantly looking for new ways to improve himself and learning new aspects of oral surgery. When he starts his own dental practice, he'll be able to tell his patients that he knows about pain and tell them stories from his Tough Mudder, like what it feels to get zapped by an electrical wire. That should make them relax and trust him.

DONALD KANNENBERG

57, Avon, Connecticut

"Trying to stay young and turn back the clock."

Don kicks off our interview by describing someone he knows as having an obsessive-compulsive nature because he rides his bike to work in all types of weather. This is coming from someone who at fifty-seven has completed two Tough Mudders and a Spartan Beast in his attempt to turn back the clock. And he's doing a good job at it.

Kannenberg grew up in Worcester, Massachusetts, and played base-ball in high school, his favorite sport. He took up tennis after college and took it on whole-hog. "I would say that my compulsive-obsessive nature came out with my love of tennis," he says. "I traveled through-out New England in tournaments almost every weekend during the summers in addition to playing five or six times during the week." He disliked running and would only do it to stay in shape for tennis. Five years ago he joined an early-morning boot camp group at his gym to get in better shape and try something different, as tennis was beginning to take up too much of his life. He met a wonderful group of people at boot camp that he describes as supportive, engaging, and fun to be with. He looked forward to his early-morning workouts three times a week, followed by strength training in the gym another three times a week, sometimes with the same people.

A year into his boot camp, Kannenberg decided to put his new training to a test and started looking for a goal. His trainer, Brian Gal-lagher, a former marine, suggested he check out obstacle course racing. He'd never heard of it, so he looked it up online and got interested in Tough Mudders. "It piqued my interest," he recalls. "I liked the chal-lenge."

With that, Kannenberg asked Brian to train him for the 2012 Tris-tate Tough Mudder event in New Jersey, which consisted of an eleven-mile course with twenty-four obstacles. He was going to do the event solo, but when word got out in boot camp about his goal, three others joined him. Kannenberg is by nature very social and engaging, so even though he initially wanted to do it alone, he welcomed the camaraderie. In honor of his friend and trainer, Kannenberg named his team Gallagher's Grunts and etched the moniker on team shirts, although during the event it didn't take long before mud left it unreadable.

Brian laid out a specific four-month training routine that included running as well as more upper-body strengthening. He had Kannenberg coming in on weekend mornings for running sessions. "I did more training than was necessary because I was afraid I wouldn't finish," he says. "The average age in these events is twenty-nine, and I was fifty-four. I didn't want to embarrass myself."

He was a little nervous as they drove to New Jersey the night before the event. "I admit to more than a few butterflies in my stomach," he recalls. He had studied all the obstacles online, including Electroshock Therapy and the Arctic Enema—a plunge into ice water—and took the tips to heart. His teammates all agreed to stay together and help one another out and took up the motto "There's no rush!"

When the event started, Kannenberg was gung-ho to conquer his first obstacle, the Arctic Enema, less than a mile into the event. The plunge into ice water shocked his system. "That sucked the life out me," he describes. He scrambled out of the container as fast as he could, cold and wet. He and his teammates were all laughing as they ran to the next obstacle. "I felt like a kid again," he says.

That's how the entire day went for Kannenberg. They'd run to the next obstacle, anxious to see what it held for them. He never felt physically challenged thanks to all his training, but there were some obstacles that the team had to come together to overcome, like the fifteen-foot warped wall. The idea is to get a running start, bound up the wall, and try to get over the top. People who have reached the top usually stay there for a while and help others over by grabbing at their extremities or whatever they can reach to pull them over. But people can get hurt, ending up with twisted wrists and wrenched elbows if someone on top pulls too much. Kannenberg's team worked together so they could make it over safely.

The tunnel was the next obstacle they faced together. This one brings out unanticipated fears in some people. The tunnels are dug into the ground and then covered in plywood, dirt, and straw. "We crawled on our bellies, bumping into walls and making wrong turns because we couldn't see anything. There is no light in the tunnel," describes Kannenberg. "We had to keep moving forward. It's like taking a leap of faith, or the blind leading the blind."

He started to realize that part of the Tough Mudder experience is addressing fears. For instance, he doesn't like heights, but when he had to jump off a platform into a pond thirty feet below, he knew his teammates were there to support him; that made it easier. He felt empowered after he accomplished the jump. "Tough Mudder makes you do things that are uncomfortable, but because your team is there to reach out and help, it makes it more palatable to go out of your comfort zone," he says. "You feel better about yourself afterward." The other realization he made is that the goal of the Tough Mudder staff is to get you as wet, cold, and muddy as possible from the get-go, so you stay uncomfortable throughout the course. There is never a time to warm up or get dry.

The last obstacle was Electroshock Therapy. One of his teammates got shocked four times, but he made it through. When Kannenberg finished the course, he felt a sense of jubilation and knew he would do another. In contrast, one of his teammates said, "One and done!"

"Doing my homework ahead of time and putting in the intense training to get in shape helped me get through this and enjoy it," he says upon reflection. His next Tough Mudder was August 2013 at Mount Snow, Vermont. He put together a new team of six, which included his trainer Brian and his wife, Ericka, along with Gary, a sixty-eight-year-old Vietnam veteran. This team was dubbed True Grit.

According to Kannenberg, this event turned into a struggle to get Gary through the course at all costs. Gary trained well, but was nervous. He studied the course from the previous year, which involved lots of traversing across the mountain, but this time around the course had been changed to mostly vertical climbs, which he struggled with. Every member of team True Grit did their part to help Gary through. At one point, Brian and Kannenberg were supporting Gary up the hill to the next obstacle at the top. Gary was spent but tried to keep moving. A young participant ran by them and then stopped, turned around, and asked Gary how old he was. When he replied, "Sixty-eight," the guy stopped in his tracks, came down to Gary, and shook his hand, saying: "You are an inspiration. Keep up the good work. I am so proud of you."

That put some needed energy into Gary's steps, and in another ten minutes they made it to the top. Waiting for them was a surprise: Fifty people, prompted by the young runner, broke out into applause and gave Gary a standing ovation. "That was a very special moment that none of us will ever forget, especially Gary," says Kannenberg. "That story has been repeated back at the gym many times to the point that Gary is now our local hero." The Mount Snow course took the team six hours to complete. They stayed together the whole way, helping and supporting one another. "We all became brothers that day," says Kannenberg.

The next event for Kannenberg was the Spartan Beast in September 2014. By then, his exploits and those of his teams were becoming the talk of the gym. He threw out the idea of putting a team together for the Spartan Beast. Says Kannenberg: "I'm not sure that was the right thing to do, to just throw it out to everyone, as the Beast is so advanced, but I did it anyway."

Five people signed up to become the Spartan Beast team. Two women, Karla, forty-eight, and Julie, thirty, had never done an obstacle course event and had no idea what they were getting into. The other members were Kannenberg, Brian, and Ericka. Kannenberg and Brian held a meeting to outline exactly what it would take to get ready. Kannenberg dubbed it The Journey.

They had nine months to train and set up their own Beast boot camp. Everyone was excited and bonded well, a good thing since they spent six days a week together sweating, running, and doing drills.

Three times a week they met from 5:30 a.m. to 7 a.m. for boot camp military drills. Two mornings a week they met for weight training, and on the weekends they went for group runs that included lots of trails and hills.

They used local playgrounds and recreational areas to simulate obstacles on the course, like the monkey bars and cargo nets. They carried fifty-pound sandbags on their shoulders and scrambled up slides. They attached a thirty-foot-long rope to a tree and practiced climbing it.

According to Kannenberg, "The Journey was so much fun. We shared lots of laughs, tears, frustrations, and hugs. And this was just the training! The girls couldn't wait to compete."

The "girls," Karla, aka K2, and Julie, aka JDog, were initially worried but "tough as nails," says Kannenberg. In late April they went on a six-mile training run up a local mountain. The day of the run was miserable: rain, sleet, and very cold. But that played in their favor, as they had to get used to adverse conditions and learned that they could conquer them. They also got used to doing Burpees, lots of Burpees.

A six-mile, fifteen-obstacle OCR in June called the Merrill Down & Dirty was the girls' entry into obstacle racing. Initially nervous, they were soon laughing and cheering along with other racers on the course. "It was incredible to see them enjoying themselves doing something so outside of the box for them," says Kannenberg.

In September, the day before the Spartan Beast, they packed the car and drove to Vermont, listening to their newly created Spartan Beast playlist that included tunes such as "Won't Back Down" and

"Hell's Bells." "Hungry," by Paul Revere and the Raiders, was a favorite. They shared idle chatter, noting a sense of nervousness in the atmosphere mixed with a bit of sadness that The Journey was almost over. As with most endurance events, the months leading up to the race are the most powerful and memorable, when friendships are forged and life experiences are created. There is a sense that in one day, all that will be over, and sadness creeps in.

Kannenberg kept the mood light and upbeat. On Friday afternoon they walked the course and saw some of the obstacles. The girls were getting nervous as they took in the size and scope of Killington. It was quite daunting.

Their wave didn't go off till 11:15 a.m., quite late. It was chilly and overcast and Kannenberg realized they would not be finishing till way after dark, but he didn't share that with the team. There were thousands of participants milling around. The elite division went off at 7 a.m. so they watched a bit of that wave compete for the prize money. Every fifteen minutes another wave of a few hundred people was released onto the course.

"The first thing I reminded our team before we started was that our goal is to stay together and finish," recalls Kannenberg. They had a support crew join them, friends from the gym who met them at various locations on the course with food, hot chocolate, and energy gels for refueling. One of the so-called Sherpas was Gary. "They were an unbelievable help to us," says Kannenberg. "They really pulled us through some rough patches with their cheering and support."

The course, fifteen miles and thirty-three obstacles, was a beast. To make matters worse, it was cold and getting dark by late afternoon. The women kept up their spirits throughout. Kannenberg felt he could actually see their strength and determination grow throughout the day instead of ebb. "They were definitely outside their comfort zone, but dug deep," he adds.

Almost ten hours later, they completed the course tired, muddy, hungry, but glowing in their achievement. "We all were in a bit of shock that we'd actually accomplished our goal, to finish this Beast." They took pictures wearing their hard-earned medals, got into some warm clothes, and headed out for a celebratory dinner. The sense of euphoria stayed with them for weeks. The first few days back at the gym, they were treated like rock stars.

Kannenberg feels that among the fundamental goals of Tough Mudders are promoting teamwork and camaraderie, and addressing your fears. The goal of Spartan is to break you mentally and physically. "Spartan did challenge us but we were prepared. Our Journey had prepared us. Karla, Julie, Don, Brian, and Ericka broke the Beast and in doing so, forged friendships for life," he says. They earned their bragging rights and the right to retell the story anytime. They all agreed that preparing for the Spartan Beast and conquering it changed their lives. Kannenberg now feels confident facing challenges that may have once been too daunting to tackle: "I've always been a person that seeks physically challenging experiences. How we deal with challenges defines us. I wasn't looking for life-altering experiences when I started doing OCRs but what I discovered with every wet, cold, muddy, and physically draining moment was a sense of empowerment to keep going; a sense of responsibility to my teammates to encourage them to scale a wall, or give a high-five after a brutally draining obstacle."

He adds: "For me there is nothing in life that compares with the camaraderie of training or participating in an OCR with a team. The Journey with my teammates in preparation for the Vermont Spartan Beast in 2014 will forever be etched in my heart and soul. The scrapes, sprains, sweat, and sore muscles were a small price to pay for the bonding and eternal friendships that evolved. The OCR was the goal, but the real reward was found in friendships."

Julie states: "I couldn't have done any of these OCRs without my teammates. In the moments at the top of the climbs, especially when I was hanging on the top of a small pole that was wobbling, I knew how easy it would be to give up—but I didn't. I wanted to conquer the challenge to join my team and continue the journey. Together, we're unstoppable!"

And Karla chimes in: "I have the bumps and bruises on my arms and legs as wonderful souvenirs of that special day in our Journey. I am so proud of us."

Karla, Julie, and Don have continued their journey together and completed a half-marathon in May, a Spartan Sprint in June and a local Down & Dirty in July. Who knows where they will go next.

MAX KING

35, Bend Oregon

"The OCR community is so welcoming.
The post-race party is the best part!"

Max King is pretty much up for anything that involves a start and a finish line, and in most cases he's the first one to cross that finish line. Co-captain of his track team at Cornell University, where he graduated in 2002, King just likes to run, and run, and run. Mostly on trails, but he'll run on any surface, anywhere. He also likes to shake it up by adding triathlons, adventure racing, cyclocross bike racing, and whatever else he finds that interests him. "If I don't shake it up, I get stale," he states. The guy's a machine. And he's so darn nice and happy and really, really fast. He also loves dark chocolate, which makes him even more likable and normal.

His résumé includes winning the IAU 100K World Championships in his 100K road race debut in 6:27:43—a 6:14 per mile average. In 2011 he claimed the World Mountain Running Championship title. He's also won the 2014 Warrior Dash championships. On the roads he holds a 2:14:36 marathon PR, 1:03:07 in the half-marathon, 29:01 in the 10K, and 14:02 in the 5K. He's so dedicated to his running that in 2008 he quit a lucrative engineering job to take a part-time job in a footwear store so he could train more. That decision has paid off not only financially—he has many sponsorship deals and puts prize money in his pocket at most races—but in lifestyle. He loves his life in Bend, running the trails in his backyard and sharing his love of the outdoors with his two kids.

In 2013, he entered the OCR arena and not surprisingly has been cleaning up there as well, winning $30,000 by placing first at the 2014 Warrior Dash World Championship, the biggest purse by far he had ever won. "That was phenomenal," he laughs. "Best payday of my sports career." That first obstacle race happened almost by default. He had planned to do a road race but it fell through so he decided to visit his mother in Medford, Oregon. When he arrived, he saw signs for an OCR five-mile event and signed up. "I'd been interested in OCRs for a while but they scared me," says King. What? Something scared the King?

He worried that he wouldn't be accepted into this new racing community, and that he wouldn't connect with them. "I'd always been a runner. Could I do this?" Basically, it was the fear of the unknown. But his engineering brain kicked in and told him that if four million people were doing it and getting through it just fine, he'd be all right. Good thing he listened.

The night before his event, he panicked. "I just about crapped my pants with nerves and didn't sleep that night. An obstacle race was something I'd been looking into for a while but way too afraid to actually sign up and do one. I always had the excuse that I had another running race that was more important and I obviously wasn't at all trained for what I was about to do," recalls King.

During that first event, he went out like the true cross-country runner he is and held second place till he needed to rely on his upper-body strength, which there was little of, for the last set of obstacles. He started to fall back. Afterward, he did a quick analysis and decided to add more pull-ups, push-ups, and core strengthening to his workout. Not much, just enough. He believes this is a runner's sport and unless he plans to do OCRs that require more upper-body strength, like the Spartan World Championships, he'll stick to his running to get to the finish first.

What's his take on OCRs? "Obstacle racing isn't for the faint of heart, it's not for someone that just wants to get through a marathon just to say they've done a marathon. If you're racing an obstacle race, it can chew you up and spit you out if you think you're just going to roll around in the mud a little. Racing one takes endurance, it takes skill, it takes efficiency of movement, and a lot of guts. That's why I'm addicted to it. Running takes you to that pain cave and I love it, but the added challenge and unknown of an obstacle race has intrigued me since it started its popular rise several years ago. Now I'm hooked and looking forward to the next year of racing."

He loves the OCR community, describing it as similar to the running community but unique all the same. When he first got into OCRs he was amazed at all the different body types, so unlike the lean runner build he was used to seeing at races. "There are these big, hulking guys at the races who could literally rip me in half," he says; he stands five foot six and weighs 135 pounds. "But they aren't intimidating at all. They are really cool guys. The OCR community is very accepting."

King, who is often referred to as America's most versatile runner, has been honored with a namesake meet, the Max King Cross Country Invitational, at his high school in Crater, Oregon. "It's quite flattering," he says. "And I'm not even dead yet." He has a lot of sponsors, including the Salomon Running Academy, GU Energy, Swiftwick socks, and Flora. He's good at promoting their lines, frequently tweeting and posting photos on social media. One former sponsor company almost named a running shoe after him. In his spare time he does online coaching and also coaches as part of Salomon. His 2015 race calendar is already full with major events like the iconic fifty-six-mile Comrades in May in Durban, South Africa; followed by the Mount Blanc Marathon in Chamonix, France, in June; a breather for the two-week running camp he sponsors for high school students; then a fifty-miler in September, defending his Warrior Dash World Championship in October, and another fifty-miler in December. And lots of other races in between all that.

So how does someone who races two to three events a month manage to stay injury-free? "With a strict adherence to stretching and strengthening," says King. He also takes a rest day and listens to his body, which most runners say they do but don't. King does. He has too much at stake not to be a smart runner.

King wants more runners to experience OCRs and thinks the Warrior Dash is a great entry into that arena. "After getting over that first experience, you can add or subtract miles and obstacles but at least you have one under your belt," he adds. "And you get that cool Fred Flintstone helmet." King gave his to his five-year-old son.

King recently posted on his runnerspace.com blog about why he does OCRs: "Doing an obstacle race is in fact a very scary proposition when you're a runner. We're not exactly known for our upper body strength, resiliency, or durability. I like to think I'm a bit of an anomaly as I can take a beating but hey, I'm still a distance runner. It's the fear of the unknown. If you've never done a running race before I could understand how that could be intimidating as well, but you know what you're going to have to do: run. But in an obstacle race every time is like your first time. You never know what is going to be thrown at you around the next corner. Your first time is nerve wracking. Are you going to have to pick up something twice your body weight, climb over a 20ft wall, swim through quicksand, or wrestle an 18ft python with just your bare hands. No, you won't."

So take it from the King. Try an OCR. You won't be sorry.

Max King's Advice for Entering OCRs

1. Don't let fear stop you from doing one. This should be fun.

2. Don't get stressed out about the obstacles. If you can't do one, go around it. No one cares. No one is judging your performance.

3. Embrace your buddies on the course. Everyone is there to have a good time, and they want to help.

4. Feel confident. You can do it.

5. Make sure to party afterward. You've earned it.

JONATHAN NAVARRO

30, Los Angeles, California

"The adrenaline rush is great!"

Jon Navarro grew up in a Chicago suburb, active and playing all types of sports since he was eight years old. In college, he formed a hip-hop dance group that competed on the national level. The intense routines helped him drop the fifty pounds he had gained since high school. But after college, his activity level fell as he worked his way up in the competitive field of architecture. In 2010, his doctor gave him a wake-up call.

His tests were not good. He had high cholesterol and high blood pressure, he smoked, and he had put himself under a lot of pressure to succeed in a new job. He was only twenty-five. His reaction was to change his lifestyle, start running, and "jump-start my fitness journey," recalls Navarro. He set a goal of running the 2011 Chicago Marathon. "I decided to run the marathon after watching my friend run it in 2010. A month and a half before race day, I injured my IT band and went through physical therapy to be as ready as I could be come race day. I finished in pain, but nothing was going to stop me from crossing the finish line. I decided to join a personal training gym to become stronger, build more muscle mass, and increase my muscle endurance in order to PR in my next marathon."

He made friends at the gym, and some of them had done an obstacle course race. They made it sound like so much fun that he decided to try one. He chose a Warrior Dash in June 2012 in South Illinois and entered with his girlfriend. He didn't add any new training; he felt fit from his marathon and circuit training at the gym, and he just wanted to experience it. "I loved it!" he exclaims. "It was so much fun and the party at the end was amazing." He finished in the top twenty-five overall and couldn't wait for the next one. A month later he ran the 2012 Chicago Marathon, achieving a personal best and shaving seventeen minutes off his previous finishing time.

With one OCR behind him and knowing what to expect, he upped the ante and entered a Tough Mudder in 2013 with group of friends.

"That was extremely challenging, but also extremely fun," says Navarro. "After that race, I felt like I needed to see where my physical fitness stacked up." He chose a Spartan Super in Illinois, 2013, for his next challenge. To prepare, he researched videos and YouTubes of Spartan courses and obstacles. He read reviews and learned how the pros trained. He changed his training and went outdoors, running on trails and rugged terrain. He dragged tires and cement blocks, climbed on monkey bars, and carried weights on his shoulder while running on the treadmill. He set a goal of finishing in the top two hundred overall and felt it was attainable. Although Spartan events can be team-oriented, he entered alone. "I wanted to test myself and rely solely on me," says Navarro. The only issue he worried about was his shoulders. They had dislocated in high school when he was playing basketball and baseball, and they occasionally still nagged him.

The Spartan Super was going to be challenging, eight to ten miles of rough terrain and twenty-four to twenty-nine obstacles, but he felt prepared and ready. At the event, there were only three obstacles he could not conquer. The spear throw didn't go well. As Navarro points out, "That's one obstacle that you can't really duplicate on your own!" He also had trouble pulling concrete blocks up the hill and chose to do Burpees instead. The rope climb to ring the bell didn't go smoothly, either, even after three attempts. "I didn't wear gloves and the rope was so slippery from all the mud residue, I gave up," he states. "I was fine doing the Burpees."

At the end, he reached his goal, finishing 133rd out of roughly

2,000 participants. "I felt great about my performance; it's a terrific sense of accomplishment." Later that year he moved to Los Angeles. He still works out at a gym and stays fit, but settling into his new architecture firm leaves little time to train for another event. "I need to get back into OCRs," he says. "I miss the adrenaline rush!" He has a Tough Mudder and a Spartan Race coming up.

Summing up his reasons for staying in the OCR community, Navarro says: "OCRs are a great way to get in shape, stay in shape, and also give you a sense of accomplishment when you set that goal and make it happen. It gives you confidence that you can carry with you throughout your life."

Navarro plans to do OCRs as long as he can and as long as his body holds up. He is inspired by the older guys who pass him on the hills and conquer the obstacles he can't. "I hope to be that older guy someday passing the young rookies!" he concludes. "That is a goal worth pursuing."

RANDY PIERCE

48, Nashua, New Hampshire

"The choices I made after going blind defined my life."

Since going blind in 1989, Randy Pierce has run four marathons, including winning the National Championship in the B1 (totally blind) division at the California International Marathon; has twice scaled all forty-eight New Hampshire mountains over four thousand feet; has been invited to the White House; and plans to climb Mount Kilimanjaro. In 2014, Pierce became the first blind American to complete a Tough Mudder obstacle course. And then he went back for more.

Randy Pierce loves his home state of New Hampshire. He was always active, running through the woods, a Boy Scout, a member of his high school band—anything that would take him away from homework. He continued on to the University of New Hampshire. After college he worked as a computer hardware designer and took up fencing. One day in class, his instructor noticed that his blind spot was oddly enlarged—actually three times the size of a normal blind spot. "You need to go to the doctor," his instructor said. "Now." He did and the diagnosis shocked him. Within two weeks, at the age of twenty-two, he had lost all the sight in his right eye, and half the sight in his left. "That instructor actually saved my sight," adds Pierce. "Because I got diagnosed right away and started treatments, I was able to save some of my central vision for eleven more years." He spent six weeks in the hospital getting tests every day with high doses of steroids pumped into him to reduce the swelling in his optic nerve.

Not a quitter, he found ways to continue his love for sports, even playing darts. He got a guide dog, Ostend. He followed the New England Patriots faithfully. He took up karate to improve his focus and orientation. But at age thirty-nine, the neurological disease that attacked his eye attacked his cerebellum, destroying his balance and landing him in a wheelchair.

"I was angry, frustrated, depressed," states Pierce. "I became that bitter person." A nurse noticed the change in him and said, "You don't want to be that person. Be the person you were, the charismatic, positive guy we met when you arrived." That was his wake-up call. "I ruminated on what she said and made a list of all the things I wanted to do and how I would do them." He spent the following "one year, eight months, and twenty-two days" in the wheelchair mapping out his goals. First on his list was to be the first blind hiker to summit all of New Hampshire's four-thousand-footers. But there was lots of work to do before he reached that goal.

"Believing you can is the first step," says Pierce, who is a sought-after speaker with a great sense of humor. He describes trying to hold on to the leash of his guide dog while pulling himself out of his wheelchair in an attempt to walk. "So here I am in a wheelchair holding on to a leash with one hand and in the other hand holding a cane for when I hopefully got up. I ended up spinning in circles!" He was transferred to the Lahey Clinic in Massachusetts for more tests. At first, the doctors thought Pierce's condition was permanent, but they ended up performing six surgical procedures. Somewhere between the second and third, they had Pierce standing on lofstran forearm crutches. His brain was healing. By the sixth procedure, they were trying to get him to stand up with the help of a stick. A normal walking stick wasn't long enough for Pierce, who's six foot four, so they gave him a hiking stick.

With lots of physical therapy and up-to-date treatments that included the BrainPort, an assistive device for the blind and visually impaired, he started walking with the hiking stick. But then another devastating setback hit Pierce when his beloved dog Ostend died from a malignant tumor. "I got angry all over again. How much could I take? This was my companion, my best friend," he recalls with lingering sadness. But he fought through his loss and got back on track.

In 2012, with his second guide dog, Quinn, by his side, he accomplished his goal in a single winter season—the winter season offering fewer challenges in terms of footing—and then on August 24, 2013, with Quinn at his side, he completed it again during the summer season.

"I didn't choose to go blind. But the choice I made after going blind, that's what defined my life. I'm not 'a blind person.' I'm a person who does all the things he wants to—and that's all because of the choice I made. The choice you make in how to respond to adversity will have a bigger impact on your life than the adversity ever could," says Pierce.

In 2014, he ran a half-marathon with a friend, Laura. She told Pierce she wanted to do an OCR and asked him to join her in Maine that August for the Great Northeast Tough Mudder. Pierce immediately jumped at the chance and said, "Let's make it happen." He searched online for any other blind person who had done an obstacle course race and found one in Australia. He studied as much as he could. But he was nervous. This would be his toughest challenge to date. "The risk of injury would be huge," he says. "I'd be on terrain that's uneven, rocky, muddy, slippery." He studied the obstacles online, figuring out how he would overcome them. His engineering background helped him figure out how to get over or under each obstacle. "I had good core strength. I would use my cane and rely on my team, whom I trust implicitly. The only thing missing was my sight!" says Pierce with his humor. "But you can have vision without sight, and I used my vision as described to me by my team."

On the morning of the Tough Mudder, his team, Team Randy ("That was not my idea!" says Pierce), didn't know what to expect. People were saying, "Let's see how far the blind guy gets." Was he anxious? Yes. Fearful? No. "I'm not a risk taker," explains Pierce. "I'm a problem solver. I felt confident I could get through this." Using his hands as his eyes, he guided himself through the obstacles with the support of his team. But then came the King of the Swingers, an obstacle that 90 percent of the participants fail. In this obstacle, he had to swing out on a T-bar eight feet across from a platform twenty-five feet above muddy water, ring a bell, then drop into the water. Hitting the bell was the difficult part. Using his engineering background, he tried to calculate by count how long he would be in the air before he reached the bell and where the bell was by listening to it ring before his turn. He used his cane to feel for where the T-bar was, to form a mental image of it, and relied on friends' descriptions of where the bell was hanging. When it came his turn, the crowd went wild with anticipation. When he succeeded, they chanted his name. The moment has been captured on a video that has gone viral. "That was an amazing moment," says Pierce. "To come up from the muddy water and hear my name being screamed by the crowd . . . I'll never forget that."

In March 2015 Pierce was selected by Oberto Beef Jerky as one of its heroes of summer; the firm sponsored his trip to a second Tough Mudder race in California. This time, his team wore T-shirts with the slogan, "I See No Obstacles." One month later he ran the Boston

Marathon in 3:50. He was a part of Team With a Vision, which supports the Massachusetts Association for the Blind and Visually Impaired. He ran to raise money and to make a point, about what he calls ability awareness. "We all have disabilities, things that we can't do. I think it's so much more important to put the focus of our lives on things we can do."

His life is now a whirlwind of speaking engagements, commencement speeches, and more endurance events, like climbing Mount Kilimanjaro in September 2015. For Pierce, 2014 will go down as a banner year with four marathons and three Tough Mudders, plus setting up his foundation, 2020Vision, which has raised $124,000 in four years. "I love my guide dogs and couldn't get along without them. It costs $51,000 to train a guide dog. I want to help ensure that anyone who needs a guide dog, gets one," he says.

Pierce has a simple philosophy: "Having a little challenge can bring out the best in people." He has challenged himself with seemingly insurmountable goals and has achieved every one with grace and humor. Where a lot of people would give up or back down, he rises. He lives his life to be the best he can be. And that's a message worth passing along.

For more information on Pierce, visit , the site of the nonprofit Pierce formed to raise funds for the guide-dog school Guiding Eyes for the Blind and the New Hampshire Association for the Blind. His Tough Mudder video can be seen on the Oberto Heroes of Summer Campaign website.

MARGARET SCHLACHTER

32, Salt Lake City

"OCRs let you play like a kid and experience life unedited."

Margaret Schlachter has had many careers in her life but none as rewarding as what she is doing now, blogging and writing about OCRs. She entered the OCR arena early, completing the first-ever Spartan Race at the Catamount Center outside Burlington, Vermont, in 2010. That race changed her life. She made all the rookie mistakes but came away charged up like never before. Since then, Schlachter has competed in close to a hundred races, including the first World's Toughest Mudder in 2011 and endurance runs of fifty-plus miles. She founded the award-winning blog *Dirt in Your Skirt*, which led to a book contract. After being a pioneer of the sport, she doesn't compete as much—she's down to fifteen events a year from a previous average of thirty—but she still likes a challenge. The main difference is that she doesn't want to suffer anymore. "I've done it the hard way, now I just want to have fun," says a more relaxed Schlachter.

Schlachter grew up in Saratoga, New York, spending most of her time around horses, as her family has been involved in the horse-racing business for three generations. Her family loved sports and the outdoor life in upstate New York, spending weekends and summers in the Adirondacks. By age two, she was skiing, "gently pushed down the hill by my father," laughs Schlachter. She took to skiing like a duck to water and by ten was racing. Her parents sent her to Stratton Mountain School, a boarding school in Vermont for aspiring ski racers and national champions. Schlachter looks back on those years fondly: "I worked hard and learned by age fourteen that structure, discipline, and goal setting were key tools to anything you wanted to achieve in life." She went on to Babson College in Boston, where she continued to ski race and was also the lacrosse goalie. After graduating in 2005, she returned to Saratoga as the ski coach and assistant lacrosse coach at Skidmore College.

When a job at Stratton Mountain School opened up, she jumped at the opportunity. But a few years later she became restless. "I was on an educational track, working in schools, and really didn't give much thought to whether I was happy or not," says Schlachter. Like the lyrics from the Talking Heads song "Once in a Lifetime," she wondered: "How did I get here? My God, what have I done?" And when she really dug deep, she realized she was miserable but didn't have a Plan B.

Her career took an unexpected turn when the 2008 economic downturn led to budget cuts at Stratton Mountain School. "I was becoming a casualty of my alma mater, the same school that established a citizenship award in my name and where I had worked in admissions for the past three years," she writes in the introduction of her training book, *Obstacle Race Training*. Her world as she knew it was crumbling. She continues: "I numbed my emotions looking down a bottle at night and hiking away the hangover in the morning." She packed on twenty pounds, forgoing her healthy athlete's diet for wings and $2 drafts. After a year of being in a state of emptiness, her epiphany came one night when she was stopped by the police and tested for alcohol. She failed the Breathalyzer test. As she describes: "The kind police officer took pity on me and offered me a second chance at a field sobriety test. As the rain poured down, I carefully listened to the instructions and did as he said. I passed and realized I had dodged the biggest bullet of my life. It was at this moment I knew I had to make a change."

She took the gift of a second chance seriously. She started a new job at a new school, stopped partying, and looked for a healthier way to blow off steam. She found it while browsing Facebook on a wintry evening in early 2010. "A newsfeed for a new event called the Spartan

Race popped up," she recalls. "The race was advertised as a two-mile trail run with obstacles. It said you would get wet and muddy. *Maybe this is what I am looking for.*" The event was less than two hours away in Burlington. The thought of competition was appealing as well. She had spent her post-college life coaching other student athletes and now had an opportunity to get back in the game.

She showed up on race day not knowing what to expect. Even though she made mistakes and felt like she didn't know what she was doing, she loved it. "The spark of my inner competitor was relit. It was time for me to regain who I was and discover who I could be," she recalls. What she ultimately discovered and embraced was the OCR world. Never a runner, she picked up trail running, ran some 5Ks, and signed up for her next OCR, a ten-mile Tough Mudder. "I was nervous at the start, wondering what I had gotten myself into," she recalls. She plunged in head-on, finishing as the third woman at the Mount Snow Tough Mudder in the first heat and qualifying for the first World's Toughest Mudder in December 2011 in New Jersey. The same day she registered for the event, she started her blog, Dirt-InYourSkirt.com, a personal account discussing her races, her training and workout logs, and her moods. "The blog helped to keep me accountable for my training," she explains. "It became my journey." People took notice, and her audience grew. No one was doing what Schlachter was doing.

To prepare for Worlds, she did a Spartan Beast, placing as the third woman overall. She followed that up with a Warrior Dash podium finish and then placed sixth in the first Spartan Race World Championships in Texas. A few weeks later she was in New Jersey for World's Toughest Mudder, an event that would go down in OCR history as epic due to frigid temperatures that doomed 90 percent of the field. By midnight, the water obstacles were covered in ice, and all the other obstacles were coated in a thin sheet of it. She lasted twenty-one hours and completed almost forty miles before extreme hypothermia caused her to drop out. Only two other women stayed out on the course and completed the full twenty-four hours.

By now her OCR résumé had caught the attention of sponsors, and she was getting some money. With those endorsements, she took a leap of faith and quit her job to go full-time, becoming the first professional female obstacle course racer. Later that same day, she received an email that would further change her life and set her on a new path. A publisher who followed her blog asked her to write a book on OCRs. The time had come for OCRs to step up in the sports world, and she was the prefect person to tap for the job. She still recalls her early years in the sport, coming to work after an event with bruises, limping into the office. "No one asked to see my medal or ask how it went. They just thought what I did was crazy," she remembers. "But if someone had run a marathon, they were all in awe, wanted to see the medal and talk about their achievement." She vowed to change that.

She took another leap of faith and moved to Salt Lake City in 2012 with her boyfriend, Forest, leaving the East Coast and everything familiar to her behind.

For most of 2012 and 2013, she competed at the top of her game, wrote her training book, and further developed *Dirt in Your Skirt* as an empowerment tool for women of all abilities to explore new possibilities and conquer their fears. By 2014, she was becoming—by choice—less the competitive athlete and more the expert with her book and blog. Schlachter has come a long way from that night sitting in the police car thinking her life was in ruins. She and Forest have a house with gorgeous views of the mountains; a garden where they pick kale, tomatoes, spinach, and other greens for dinner; multiple beehives where they hope to get honey; and a peaceful contentment. Forest forages for mushrooms in the mountains, which they will put in a pasta. She finds it awkward to see herself as a pioneer of women's OCR, despite the fact that she was one of the first to pursue the sport and make a name for herself. It's not a role that comes naturally, but like it or not, she is an inspiration for the next generation of girls and women getting into the sport. Think of her as a female Tony Hawk.

Happily ensconced in Salt Lake City, she spends her time writing about OCRs on her blog, as editor in chief for MudRunGuide.com, and in her column on About.com. When she does compete, she's found a balance: "I make it challenging but I don't want to suffer through pain anymore!" She's most stoked when helping others navigate their way through the crazy world of OCRs. She's funny, open, spirited. She dedicated her book to her family for their encouragement throughout her journey and their unwavering support. How appropriate, as that is exactly what Schlachter gives to everyone she meets.

VIV SCHOELLER

63, Wayne County, Pennsylvania

"Mom's a badass!"

Vivian Schoeller: gutsy, full of grit, and the oldest woman to participate in the Spartan Sprint, in Tuxedo, New York, on June 6, 2015. It's her first-ever obstacle course race. She's also registered for the Spartan Super in July, and the Spartan Beast just two months later in September in Killington, Vermont. Almost five foot four, her graying hair pulled back in a ponytail, her arms inked with her race number, and sporting a smile, Schoeller walks around the base of the ski slope like a kid at camp. Younger entrants, especially those with kids, stop her and ask for a photo. Not many believe this sixty-three-year-old will conquer the course, one of the toughest sprint courses on the circuit with close to five miles of up-and-down rocky, slippery trails and twenty-two obstacles. Four hours later, Schoeller proves she is indeed a badass, just one with a gray ponytail, a big smile, and covered in stinky mud.

Schoeller grew up in the countryside in Connecticut, an only child. "Since the age of three, my playmates were our dog and the cows and my horse," she says. "My dad taught me at an early age to be responsible, have discipline, and persevere." During World War II, her dad was in the army and trained homing pigeons, which were still in use. The work of homing pigeons was so important to the war effort that in England, the , the highest possible decoration for valor given to animals, was awarded to thirty-two pigeons, including the US Army Pigeon Service's G.I. Joe and the Irish pigeon Paddy. After the war, her father kept homing pigeons and raced them for sport. She was in charge of recording the flight times of the pigeons when they arrived back at the coop. At age six, she was climbing up the ladder to the top of the barn, whistling in the pigeons, taking off their bands, and clocking and recording their flight times. Her dad gave her other chores around the house such as training their pet Doberman to bring in the newspaper. After high school she attended dog-grooming school. She was so comfortable around the animals that she went on to become a trainer and learned many lessons that she could apply to her own life. She studied Karen Pryor, who became famous for her work known as "clicker training," basically positive reinforcement. "You can't force animals, or anyone, to do something they don't want to do," explains Schoeller. "You need to shape the behavior with positive reinforcement, which sets the training up for success, not failure." She applied those lessons to her own life. As a dog handler she won numerous awards. She also volunteered to train Seeing Eye puppies with the 4-H Club.

She moved to Honesdale, Pennsylvania, in search of a less expensive place to live and eventually got a job as a cashier at the local Walmart. She continued to work with dogs, taking in a retired Seeing Eye dog, and enjoyed working in her garden. She met Randy Weller, also sixty-three, a multiple Spartan Trifecta winner and ranked number one in his age group internationally and in the United States. He introduced her to Spartan races. After watching him at an event, she thought, *I could do that.* The timing was perfect, because her beloved dog Boomer, a rottweiler rescue dog from Hurricane Katrina, had just died and she needed something to take up her time. Now set on doing her first OCR, she needed to improvise a training circuit, as she didn't have the budget to join a gym.

"It's amazing what you can find in the neighborhood," she laughs. Piece by piece, she added equipment. She found a free treadmill from a family that was moving; a weight bench and a mountain bike at a garage sale. She found a stepper, and two high-backed chairs for triceps dips. She went on Facebook and found weights. She went to Goodwill and got a stability ball. She bought a bucket at Home Depot and filled it with fifty-pound sandbags. She studied videos of obstacles and tried to figure out how she would do them. She ran through the hills in her neighborhood. She did planks and push-ups. She was prepared!

What was driving her to start competing in obstacle course races at age sixty-three was something beyond her *I can do this* mentality. "I don't want to be the frumpy, dumpy, grumpy, senior citizen who everyone passes by, invisible to anyone under thirty," she says. "I much prefer to be the crazy senior citizen who shakes it up and believes she can do anything!" And by *anything*, she meant business, signing up for a Spartan Sprint, Super, and Beast at the same time. That spirit of adventure would serve her well at the events.

With limited money to spend on traveling or for lodging, she went online to the Spartans of the Northeast website and found a supportive group of women. One offered her a ride to Killington in September. "I found the OCR community so welcoming," says Schoeller. "No one cared how old I was or questioned my ability to do this." She volunteered at an event in May, which gave her a free pass to the Spartan Sprint in Tuxedo in June, on a Saturday, then volunteered on Sunday for her free entry to the Spartan Super in July. "Volunteering is so much fun," says Schoeller. "You meet great people."

The morning of the event, Schoeller walked around the base area taking it all in, studying the course map, and soaking up the electric atmosphere, despite the rain. She was going to do her best and give it her all. She had to take a vacation day from work to be there. On her wrist was a series of wristlets; a purple one for women Spartans over forty, a red one for Spartans of the Northeast, and the free beer wristlet. She was ready to go. Randy was with her, but had a different wave start. When he could spot her on the course, he shouted encouragement.

The course, 4.7 miles and twenty-two obstacles, was challenging. When she got to the Tarzan Swing, rumors were circulating that people were spraining or, worse, breaking ankles. "I watched people before me and made a quick study that I needed to grasp the rope as high as I could and tuck my knees up high as well," she says. "Then I closed my eyes and pushed off!" She took her time on the steep, slippery trails though the woods, not wanting to be a hero as she watched others slip and fall onto the rocks and exposed roots. The rope climbs were difficult, as she doesn't have a lot of upper-body strength. "I made it to the first knot and that was as far as I got, but at least I gave it a try," she states. "I did my share of Burpees and have to say I did them much better than some of the women half my age." She missed a total of six obstacles and finished in four hours. At one point on the course she heard her name being called out by the announcer. Not realizing they were giving her a shout-out, she thought she had done something wrong. "Was I dying? Was I being thrown off the course?" Schoeller laughs a lot, and you find yourself laughing along and, better yet, cheering for her at every step.

When she finally jumped over the fire pit and crossed the finish line, she was thrilled. "I was so proud of myself," she cries. "It felt so good." Later on she found out she was the oldest woman on the course. If she completes the upcoming Beast, she could be the oldest woman to earn the Spartan Trifecta medal. She's already put in for those vacation days.

Schoeller has met a whole new world of friends since she entered the world of Spartan races. "Everyone is so friendly and helpful," she says. "I have a very exciting life. People treat me with respect at the events when they find out how old I am. Here, I'm not invisible. I'm getting new 'friend' requests every day!"

It's been proven that as we age we need to keep busy, have interests, be active, and socialize. Throughout her life, Schoeller has been all these things, but she realizes now more than ever she can't stop. "Thank goodness I found Spartan races," she exclaims. After finishing her first sprint, she feels on top of the world. She won her age division, her son thinks she's a badass, her friend Randy is proud of her. Her three-year-old grandson does Burpees with her. Schoeller sums up life in her mid-sixties: "I'm happy and having the time of my life!"

AMANDA SULLIVAN

36, Atlanta, Georgia

"Finding hope when all seems hopeless."

Amanda Sullivan has been an athlete all her life. She was captain of her varsity field hockey, basketball, and lacrosse teams in high school, where she was named Female Athlete of the Year. At Villanova University, she played club and intramural sports. She's trained in white-water rafting and rock climbing. Not only does she have the discipline of a top-ranked athlete, she has the heart of a giver and caretaker. After college she was an aid worker for orphans, refugees, and abused women and children in South America, living in Costa Rica, Chile, Panama, Jamaica, and Mexico. But as Amanda tells it, God decided to take her on a different, although just as challenging, journey in December 2008 that ultimately left her disabled. But like the mythical Phoenix she rose up stronger than ever, with her determination and humor intact. She became a Spartan Warrior, the first woman in the world with a physical disability to earn the Trifecta medal for completing each of the three main Spartan Race courses in one calendar year.

The day her life changed, she was sitting in her car waiting to make a turn when a driver who was texting hit her from behind. The accident left her with a fractured skull, broken nose, traumatic brain injuries, and a severely sprained neck and back as well as sprained and strained arm muscles. She was bedridden for five weeks, suffering daily post-traumatic migraines. Her only thought was how she was going to get back to Mexico to open a new orphanage. Finally cleared to begin physical therapy, she was walking into the hospital for her first visit when she was run over by a man who accidentally put his car in reverse, stepped on the gas, and slammed into her. Sullivan can recall the impact: "I was struck on my right side and tossed up onto the back of the car, cracking the right side of my head on his back windshield. I got shot off the car and cracked my head a few times on my left side. I ended up pretty much injuring everything from my skull to my toes." She suffered more brain injuries and ripped just about every muscle, ligament, and tendon in her body. Doctors discussed amputating her right leg. Always the fighter, Sullivan reacted with discipline and drive: "That scary news turned my beast mode switch to 'on.' I began doing double sessions of physical therapy the next day."

Despite her strong desire to get better, she fell into a deep depression partly due to her traumatic brain injuries and the news that she would be permanently disabled. She had already undergone back-to-back surgeries in 2009 and spent a total of three years in bed, and now she was confined to a wheelchair. "I started isolating myself," she recalls. "It was difficult to think clearly while being in constant pain and I felt like I couldn't really open up to anyone because no one understood what I was going through. I realized that I needed to focus on what made me happy and simply avoid anything that could hurt me. I went into survival mode and thought about all the things I would do when I was better." She created a poster board in her hospital room and filled it with sticky notes of all the things she wanted to accomplish. She called it her "hope board." She also reached out to other disabled athletes on Facebook and found a supportive and nurturing community of wounded military veterans at Walter Reed Hospital who convinced her to join a gym and start living life.

It was just what she needed to lift herself out of her depression. "The day I played wheelchair basketball for the first time, a part of my soul that I thought was gone was reborn," says Sullivan. "When I started going out and doing fun things again, I began making new memories with this new body of mine. Sometimes our bodies need to break in order for our souls to be healed." She stayed in touch with her wounded warrior friends at Walter Reed, and one in particular, Corporal Todd Love, a marine who'd lost both legs above the hip and an arm in a bomb explosion. They encouraged her to use forearm crutches to transition out of the wheelchair and slowly work her way to using a hand cycle machine and a treadmill at the gym. Already smitten with Corporal Love, she did everything that was suggested, never guessing there was a hidden agenda to their encouragement.

That agenda was to get Sullivan to complete the Tunnels to Towers 5K race in September 2012. When they suggested it to her and said they would come up and do it with her, she gladly accepted the challenge. "I had a crush on Todd so I thought, well, I might die during this race, but at least I'll get to hang out with Todd before I die," she says, laughing.

She was nervous about the event, worried that she would be lost in the throng of more than thirty thousand runners or, worse, that people would make fun of the young woman in pigtails walking with forearm crutches on crooked legs. Instead, thousands of firefighters, military personnel, spectators, and onlookers cheered her. She finished last but was most likely the happiest finisher. Two of her wounded military friends, triple amputees, walked alongside her. "It ignited a fire within my heart that will never be snuffed. Their vibrant spirits, courage, and smiles were contagious," recalls Sullivan.

She and Todd Love have been together ever since. Love introduced her to a whole new world of sports. They've gone skydiving, and Love surfs and skis.

After that race, Sullivan raised the bar and went crazy signing up for races. She signed up for her first Spartan Sprint in July, followed by a Spartan Super in August, in Virginia. Sullivan reached out to her friend and coach Alex Nicholas, a member of the Spartan Pro Team, to help her through the race. That Sullivan would choose a Spartan Super—whose course winds up and down a steep ski slope—is testimony to her strength and courage. Or that she's just crazy determined. Both are true. As Nicholas recalls: "Most everyone had trouble coming down, as the trail was steep, rocky, and not easy to maneuver. I worried she would wipe out, but she didn't. Every step of the way she surprised me with her grit and how she uses her body to compensate for things she can't do. Like stuffing sandbags in her backpack to get through that obstacle since she can't use her hands. She loves to drag the cement blocks as she has very strong upper-body strength. She does her share of Burpees. She surprised me every step of the way." Completing the Spartan Super took a lot out of Amanda but it proved she was more than capable of handling an obstacle course.

"At first, I wasn't sure if I could finish the race. But with each step I took, I learned that it's not about being in first place, or last place, or looking a certain way or having a certain body. These races are about encouragement, friendship, celebrating life, shining in the face of adversity, and overcoming odds," says a renewed Sullivan.

With a Sprint and a Super completed, she was ready to rest. But then she received a call from the Spartan organizers. They had been following her progress and suggested if she wanted to complete the

Trifecta that year, there was only one Beast left: in Dallas, Texas, in December, the following weekend. If Sullivan agreed to be videoed for the event, they would pay all her expenses. They happened to mention that no disabled woman had ever completed a Beast. And to sweeten the pot, they offered to pick up the expenses to board her beloved puppy. There was just one caveat: the weather. A cold front was moving into the area, with temperatures plummeting into the low twenties.

Sullivan called Love, who was skiing in Colorado at the time, and talked it over with him. He bluntly said she would probably die on the course and it wasn't a good idea. But she thought of the kids who follow her on social media and how she is always telling them you don't have anything to prove by finishing; just starting is good enough. She knew she had to give it a try. "I wouldn't let my fear get in the way," she says.

The one person she knew would help was Nicholas. He jumped on a plane and met her in Dallas, which as predicted was twenty-seven degrees. This was going to be the toughest thing she had ever done in her life but she was not going to back down. "I didn't come here to skip obstacles," she says with defiance. "I don't want to die but I'm not going to quit, either." She praised the support and ingenuity of Nicholas. "He'd come up with the most amazing ways for me to get through, under, or over an obstacle," she states with pride in her coach. But one obstacle, a thirty-foot slippery wall, almost did her in. To reach the top, participants use a rope to pull themselves up. Nicholas went first and waited for her at the top to pull her over. Sullivan climbed up the slippery wall on the rope to the point where she could grab Nicholas's hand. Before he could pull her over, though, she could feel her hand slipping out of the glove. As she recalls: "It just took seconds, but in those seconds we locked eyes knowing what was happening and I said, 'This is going to be bad' and with that my hand slipped completely out of the glove. I flipped over backward and went crashing off the side of the wall, breaking my ribs and hitting my head so hard I was unconscious." Everyone tried to get her to go to the medical tent and quit.

But Sullivan was not to be deterred and went back out and made it over the wall in her next attempt. By now, extremely fatigued, her mud-covered face barely visible beneath her ski cap, Sullivan still flashed her signature smile. She could see the fire pits at the finish line and knew she would make it. "Everyone kept telling me to concentrate really hard on the flames and try to look through the flames for inspiration," recalls Sullivan. "I looked really hard and couldn't believe my eyes. Todd was there." Love had driven from Colorado to surprise her and was waiting with her Trifecta medal and a cup of hot chocolate at the finish line. "That was the best memory I will ever have in my life," says Sullivan.

Winning that Trifecta was the highlight of her life. The second biggest highlight was giving it away. Sullivan has a hundreds of followers on her Facebook page and she diligently keeps up with them. She started connecting with parents of an eight-year-old girl named Elizabeth was has spina bifida and had been using forearm crutches until a bunch of mean kids at school started making fun of her. She switched to a wheelchair to avoid the cruel remarks. When her parents found Sullivan's website, they asked her to reach out to their daughter as a role model, and to encourage her to keep walking. Sullivan did that, and more. She befriended Elizabeth, encouraging her to use her forearm crutches and to start taking charge of her young life. Elizabeth was in awe of Sullivan, and to live up to her mentor she entered a Spartan kids' race. For months, Sullivan talked her through her training, her frustrations, her ups and downs. She sent Elizabeth a pair of her signature Superman socks to wear at the event. And then she flew out to the race to surprise her, and they did the event side-by-side. When Elizabeth finished, Sullivan placed her Trifecta medal around her neck. "I wanted to teach Elizabeth that just because she has a disability, she shouldn't let that define who she is or be treated any differently. I wanted to show her that she has no limitations and to make the most of every day," recalls Sullivan. The medal came with the caveat that Elizabeth will pass it on to another person that she inspires to help through adversity. In a gesture of thanks to her role model, on the sixth anniversary of her accident Elizabeth sent Sullivan a doll, a customized action-figure Sullivan look-alike, complete with the Superman socks.

She doesn't stop challenging herself. In 2014, she used her forearm crutches to complete the Marine Corps Marathon in just over seven hours. She broke all her toes dragging her feet along but didn't stop. She dedicated the 26.2 miles to the men in Love's marine platoon who helped save his life.

Sullivan is still undergoing treatment and has more surgeries to go. Her right leg will probably never function. She will always suffer debilitating migraines from the traumatic brain injuries. Her bulging and herniated disks will continue to poke through and create havoc with her spinal cord. Miraculously, her teeth were not injured in either accident so she keeps her radiant smile through it all. Says Sullivan: "I took this as a direct sign from the universe to keep smiling no matter what."

Sullivan has been named to the Spartan Pro Team—its first female adaptive athlete. She hopes this will open the door for many more adaptive athletes in the future. Future plans include a repeat of the Tunnels to Towers 5K, followed by walking the Marine Corps Marathon. She's also learned to let go of any anger or resentment against the two men who caused her injuries. "Forgiveness is part of the healing process," she states. "Life is too short to feel like a victim or to focus on the people who have hurt me. I would rather feel the light and hope and love that engulfs my soul than anger."

Sullivan and Love live their lives to the fullest. Nothing stops them from achieving their goals and dreams. "We are in a position to help others with adapted abilities to see their opportunities, especially kids," says Sullivan. " When we all work together there isn't anything we can't achieve."

LOUIS VAZQUEZ

55, Brooklyn, New York

"I'm a changed man."

Lou Vazquez's mild manner and engaging smile belie the fierce competitor that lies beneath. He's a dedicated family man who has worked hard all his life. He has a dream job: director of sports at Randall's Island Park Alliance, overseeing all the national and local track-and-field events that take place on this hallowed field just a stone's throw from Midtown Manhattan. The world-class Icahn Stadium, the heart of Randall's Island Park Alliance, is his office. Icahn Stadium, formerly Downing Stadium, is where Jesse Owens won the hundred-yard dash and went on to a historic win at the 1936 Berlin Olympics. It hosted the 1964 Women's Olympic Track and Field Trials, and more recently, in 2008, was the site where Usain Bolt broke the world record in the men's hundred meters during the Reebok Grand Prix, in front of a capacity crowd of seventy-five thousand spectators. This is where Vazquez, fifty-five, comes to work and play.

Vazquez's entire life has been shaped by his passion for sports and competition. He grew up in the Midwood section of Brooklyn, where his block was his first playground, site of kickball games, stoop ball matches, all the games a city kid could play in the streets. He ran track and cross-country for four years at Xaverian High School and continued at Brooklyn College, a Division III school, where he qualified for the nationals. He ran his first marathon in 1983, in 2:36.

"I've always been a competitive runner," says Vazquez. "I was lucky to have a lot of success early on." After college he coached at Bishop Ford High School, which in its heyday was a powerhouse for track-and-field competitions. He then coached for twelve years at Long Island University while getting his master's degree in sports medicine. This is definitely someone who is goal-oriented and can multitask.

He also gets his family engaged in sports. His wife, Ann, was a pioneer in women's running, already out on the road in the early 1970s. His daughter played soccer and now competes in triathlons; his son played ice hockey and baseball. "I think it is important to introduce sports to your kids and get them involved early," he says. "Open up as many doors as you can for them and see what they like and gravitate to. The health and social benefits are essential to a fulfilled lifestyle."

So why would a guy with a 2:36 marathon who loves to run take on an OCR? "I was talked into it," he laughs. "A group of my guy friends put out the challenge and I bit." He signed up for the November 2010 Tough Mudder in Englishtown, New Jersey, a twelve-mile course filled with nineteen obstacles. This was the second-ever Tough Mudder event. Course designers used the lessons learned at the inaugural event to fine-tune this one and make it even more challenging.

"My goal was to finish in one piece," says Vazquez. "There wasn't much information out there about OCRs since they were so new. I wasn't worried about the twelve miles but I was worried about the obstacles I saw online, especially the ice-water plunges." His wife and kids thought he was crazy for entering, and he had a bout of anxiety and nerves the night before. "I was very worried," he admits. "I thought I could really get hurt."

His team of fifteen buddies, mostly runners and former athletes of one degree or another, called themselves the Has Beens. Their mindset going into the event was: "I don't know why we're doing this, why we're here, not sure what obstacles we can even do, but we will stick together and make sure we all help each other and finish together."

Not entirely a good beginning! But they had a sense of humor and were up for the challenge. For Vazquez, it was something new. And he liked the idea that the event was not timed. For him, running is usually all about beating the clock; he was looking forward to focusing simply on getting to the finish line intact. It was, however, the first time he ever had to sign a death waiver and agree to take out "catastrophic insurance." The thought *I am fifty years old. Why am I doing this?* ran through his mind once again.

One of the first obstacles he faced was jumping into a pool of ice water. As he recalls: "When I hit the water my heart started to race. I was wearing Dri-Fit shorts and a T-shirt and when I got out of the water my thighs were bright red and I couldn't stop shaking from the cold. I actually thought of dropping out, less than a mile from the start!"

The second obstacle wasn't any better. He had to pull himself through a river of icy mud, then climb up to a platform fifteen feet above the river and jump back into the icy mud. He thought, *I've only gone two miles. How will I ever finish? What the heck am I doing this for?* All the Has Beens were feeling the same way, proving once again that misery does love company. They stuck together and struggled together.

The half-pike obstacle stands out in Vazquez's mind as especially brutal. The idea is to run full speed at a curved twenty-foot wall, jump and try to reach the top, and pull yourself over. It took one team member eight attempts to reach the top. Every failed attempt meant sliding back down the wall and getting friction burns all over his body.

The Has Beens moved forward, tackling each obstacle in a calculated way. They did a quick analysis of their combined strengths and weaknesses and used that to get through the course. It became clear that upper-body strength was a necessity at almost every obstacle, something Vazquez had not trained for. He was glad he didn't approach his first OCR as a competition. That gave him the leeway to bypass obstacles he didn't want to deal with, such as Electroshock Therapy. The idea of exposing his body to live electrical wires was too much for him. *That's just crazy*, he thought to himself. Tough Mudder rules state that you can bypass an obstacle, but the penalty is doing thirty Burpees.

That was the last obstacle. He did his Burpees and then raced to the finish. It took him an hour and a half in all. "I thought it was amazing that I finished—and in one piece. I met my only goal," he says.

A year later he did his second OCR. OCRs were still young; there weren't many offered in the tristate area. He searched the web for OCRs that were timed to test himself against others in his age group. The competitor in him was becoming unleashed as he made the commitment to concentrate on OCRs and give up road racing. "I didn't tell anyone I was doing this as I wasn't sure I could compete at the top and be one of the best in my age division," he says. He entered a Down & Dirty, a new entry in the OCR series. Down & Dirties offer a 5K or 10K course and use obstacles similar to Tough Mudders, but not as much icy water or electrical shocks. There is, however, lots of mud.

Vazquez ran through mud, crawled through mud, carried sandbags, and ran through the woods. It took him one hour and he placed in his age division. That was his breakthrough to feeling he could really compete in OCRs. Over the next two years he entered more Down &

Dirties, Warrior Dashes, City Challenges—any OCR event that would prepare him for more advanced and challenging courses. After each, he would analyze his strengths and weaknesses, and work on improving for the next time.

If one of the goals of participating in OCRs is to change up your life, it certainly did that for Vazquez. He created his own training regimen at Randall's Island, starting out with a six- to eight-mile run around the island, followed by sprinting up the stadium steps, doing a set of ten Burpees and ten push-ups at the top, sprinting down, and repeating this for about an hour. After a shower, he's ready to start his workday. He's become addicted to the sport, doing an OCR almost every weekend. He loves the social aspect and now finds most of the obstacles fun, though he still hates the icy water and electrical shocks. "Most of the obstacles are things we did as kids, like climbing monkey bars, balancing on a bar, or jumping rope," he says. "The difference is that as kids it was easy, but now that I am over fifty, it's not so easy!" One thing he likes about OCRs that's different from road racing is the element of surprise—the unexpected obstacle that is always a part of the course. "In a road race, you know what is involved. It's the next mile and the next. Nothing new," he explains. "I liked the idea of not knowing what was next."

In 2014 he did his first Spartan event. He was drawn to Spartan for a number of reasons, mostly because the races are timed and don't involve any ice-cold water. The course is usually a ski slope, so a lot of running is involved—but because it is mostly uphill, he feels it equalizes the field for the runners versus the CrossFit crowd. Spartan races appeal to first-timers who are just dipping their toe into OCRs. It's doable but challenging and doesn't have the extreme obstacles of a Tough Mudder.

Vazquez signed up for the Spartan Sprint in Tuxedo, New York, in May, a hilly four-mile course. The constant running up and down is interrupted by obstacles like a giant uphill mud crawl, snow guns that shoot streams of water, or crawling under barbed wire. But he miscalculated the difficulty of the course, ending up dehydrated with the dry heaves, totally exhausted. On his last run to the top, he collapsed with a hundred yards to go and just lay down on the grass. "People were stopping and asking if I was all right. I just wanted to be left alone," he says. "I finally sat up and saw a big sign that read: YOU CAN BEG. YOU CAN CRY. YOU CAN CRAWL. YOU CAN BLEED. BUT DON'T EVER GIVE UP." He got up and finished but couldn't move for an hour. "I was really hurting," he recalls. It took him two hours to complete the four-mile course. "That course beat my butt and I wasn't happy. It was an epiphany of sorts for me that I needed to up my game."

He started training harder, adding more upper-body strengthening, more hill running, more push-ups. He thought through his strategy. Seven weeks later he signed up for a Spartan Super in Vernon, New Jersey. This time, he stopped at every water station and paced himself. "It was nerve racking," he recalls. "At mile six, I thought I had hit the Wall but persevered. It was a huge challenge for me; I was always out of my comfort zone." He finished in 2:45, besting his Sprint time by a huge margin, and felt elated.

After doing more than ten OCRs, he lost interest in running. "Everything now is a surprise, a challenge, a mental puzzle, and I love that. Running didn't offer that for me." He also knew his days of setting personal bests were over, whereas OCRs offer the excitement of always trying to get better, and the thrill of succeeding. For his Super Spartan, the surprise obstacle was a pit filled with kettle balls that had to be emptied out.

To date, Vazquez has done twenty-four OCRs. During his season, August to November, he'll do one almost every weekend. He's recruited his daughter to do one with him. "I found my niche and I love it," he says. "I wish they had these around when I was younger."

His newest goal is to complete a Spartan Beast.

"I'm having so much fun! I love OCRs," he exclaims. "When I do these events I am not comparing myself to anyone. It's me against me. I'm not trying to better a time; the challenge for me is more mental than running marathons and keeps me in better shape." He goes on: "It has the endurance component, which I love from my running days, but there are challenges along the course. Anyone can run a 5K, but throw in fifteen or twenty obstacles along the way and now we have a real challenge. It's an unbelievable feeling when you cross the finish line knowing that you just did something that took you out of your comfort zone. I now carry this over to my everyday life as well as my training and feel the better for it."

Since completing his first Tough Mudder in 2010, Lou Vazquez has lost forty pounds and feels healthier then ever. Despite the dusting of gray around his temples, he fits in with the thirty-year-olds he regularly beats. He loves to talk about his OCR life and get others involved. He orchestrated a City Challenge obstacle course on Randall's Island in 2014 and would like to see more of them.

Vazquez has just one piece of advice for anyone wanting to try an OCR: Pick an easy one to start and don't get discouraged. He picked a Tough Mudder to start, got discouraged in the first mile, but had the perseverance to tough it out and finish. That's what it takes.

ISAIAH VIDAL

22, Marble Falls, Texas

"Never settle for less than you can become."

Isaiah Vidal, a member of the Spartan Pro Team, is fast becoming a legend in obstacle course racing even though it's been just four years since he exploded onto the circuit. During a weekend in September 2014, he placed sixth overall and first in his age division at the Spartan

Beast on a Saturday—and the next day won the Spartan Ultra Beast
in a time of 9:41:36. His biggest claim to fame was taking up the challenge thrown down by Spartan founder and CEO Joe DeSena to bike
from Austin, Texas, to Killington, Vermont, to compete in the 2013
Spartan World Championships after Vidal said he could not afford the
transportation. It took him sixteen days, covering 116 miles a day.
When he arrived in Vermont, he ran the Beast and finished tenth overall. But he wasn't tired yet. The following day he completed the Ultra
Beast, placing sixth overall. How does he do it? "I talk to myself," says
Vidal. "I tell myself the pain will eventually go away."

Vidal grew up in Texas, poor and always moving around, as his father, who emigrated from Mexico, did not have immigration papers.
His mother was sixteen when he was born. She worked as a bus driver
while his father did landscape jobs and anything else he could to put
food on the table for Vidal and his siblings. Isaiah learned at a young
age to take care of himself and hustle for money. At age eight he took
whatever money he had earned from odd jobs, went to Sam's Club,
and bought a ton of candy, which he then sold to the kids at school
for a $1 a bar. He also ate a lot of it; he was a fat kid. His older brother
got him into soccer to lose the weight and get in shape. He worked
hard and became a standout player, then switched to football in high
school. His dad attended all his games. On the day of Vidal's eigh-
teenth birthday, while waiting for his father to come home and celebrate, the family received the news that he had been caught and was
in jail waiting to be deported back to Mexico. Vidal was crushed; he

felt lost and abandoned. "He was looking forward to coming to my high school graduation," recalls Vidal. "What should have been a monumental day in our family was just heartbreaking for me. He was so proud of my brother and me getting an education."

Looking for something to get back his drive, he decided to try an obstacle course race, something he had seen online. His mom drove him to the event. Without any training or knowing what he was doing, he finished in the top five and decided there might be a future in this. He shed twenty pounds of his football weight to become a lean mean Spartan fighting machine and started placing in his age division at age eighteen. By twenty he was winning. But he was still poor and had very little money to travel to events or pay entry fees. However, he is stubborn, a trait he gets from his dad, and also deeply spiritual and felt something good would happen. "I truly believe anything can happen if you want it badly," says Vidal. "The power of faith is strong. God is my center of gravity and I knew he would help me." And then things started to happen. Sponsors started to take notice.

With his youthful and chiseled good looks, a thick mane of dark hair coiffed to perfection, abs of steel, and a mile-wide engaging smile, he became the poster boy for OCR, and was soon featured in magazines and Spartan ads. There's a screen shot of him posted on his Instagram page—there are hundreds of photos posted there—at the 2014 Spartan Super Race in Nevada that could be a promotion for the next Avengers movie featuring Vidal as Spartan-Man. With sponsor and prize money he was able to hire a coach and travel to more events.

His list of corporate sponsors is extensive, covering everything from nutrition products to elevation training masks. And he is a good client. His social media posts are full of photos sporting the brands. He wears a fake TitinTech tattoo on his chest that looks authentic. He was a featured pro on the first Spartan cruise in February 2015, and collected $3,000 in prize money for winning the Spartan Sprint event. And then he posted about the cruise on all his social media. The guy is not only buff and talented, he is a genius at marketing.

He trains less than eight hours a week with his favorite workout day being weight lifting. It doesn't seem that much, but he is also competing almost every weekend. He also makes sure to get in his runs, as he sees the course as 70 percent running. "It isn't about the distance, it's about the output," he says. "Any OCR fanatic can go run three miles, but it's about how fast you can actually run that 5K/10K that separates you from the other competition." His favorite workout is the Steam Room Swim: He does ten Burpees every minute on the minute for ten minutes in a steam room and then does laps in the pool, repeating for two rounds.

When he's not training or at an event, he likes to talk to schoolkids on how to overcome obstacles in their lives. With his inspiring story of overcoming an impoverished family background to making it to the podium of a Spartan Beast, he's got a great story to tell, one that resonates with kids from underserved communities like the one he came from. He also spends a lot of time posting on social media to his many fans. Vidal has a lot to say. He's extremely engaging and funny. There are a lot of blessings in his posts: "Always remember everyday is a blessing"; "Devotion to yourself and the man above is important!" That's refreshing. He's not full of himself. He'll spend time helping someone new to OCR with training plans and tips. He seems to want the world to experience OCRs and see how transforming they can be. He's passionate for sure.

He credits his father as having a huge influence in his life. He proudly states: "My father taught me right from wrong and gave me the greatest gift any son would ask for: He believes in me." When Vidal participated in the Spartan Super in Mexico City, finishing in Estadio Azteca Stadium, his dad did the course with him, an emotional finish for both of them.

Here's his post on his pre-race ritual: "Morning of the race I drink 16 oz of water followed with Beetelite in 8 oz of water. Then I shower for 10 seconds hot and 10 seconds cold for 5 mins. Get the mind right with spiritual and motivational music while getting dressed. Fuel the body 2 hours before the race with an egg omelet with bacon & veggies, jam on top with some pancakes on the side (keep it light on quantity) don't want to feel like a cow! Sip on water consistently depending on condition of weather. Show up to race site 1 hour or 1 1/2 hour before start time. Start to get mentally prepared 1 hour out and walk/jog/dynamic stretch. Listen to my favorite spiritual & motivational play list. At this point my body is fresh and ready, but not fully. 15 minutes out I eat a Snickers bar as it helps me restore any last minute sugar levels as I continue to walk around. 5 minutes out its go time and I'm soon to the start line with my head down praying for an injury-free race."

For Vidal, Spartan races have given him a way to overcome the obstacles in his life and move on from the poverty and sense of loss. "I learned to look at life differently and find the silver lining despite how bleak things can get," he says. "With faith you can do all things. None of this is about me. It's about giving glory to God."

He is currently training in Colorado and misses his family, whom he considers his biggest supporters; it's one of the many sacrifices he has made to get to where he is in the game. Vidal would love to see the sport grow and is already thinking about it becoming an Olympic event. If and when it does, you can be sure he will be there and aiming for the podium, nothing less.

Advice from Isaiah Vidal

1. Think about the reason why you are doing this, as that will set the stage for everything. Are you doing it for fun? To test yourself? As a dare? Know your reason.

2. Be realistic about setting your goal. Don't set yourself up for failure by reaching too high.

3. Get rid of your ego. There's no place for an ego at OCRs.

4. Take time to recover and rest so you can start training for the next one.

SHARON REMY

46, Ocoee, Florida

"Just call me Mud Nut."

Some people do an OCR once for the experience and never do another. For others, it's a craze and they keep going back for more. That pretty much describes forty-six-year-old Sharon Remy. She grew up in Columbus, Ohio, with an older brother, Steve, and her parents, both teachers, who were always very active. Remy has been an athlete all her life, starting with gymnastics in third grade, followed by soccer and the swim team. She learned to deal with injuries, pain, and disappointment early on when she broke bones in her feet during a routine that included a round-off, three or four back handsprings, and a final back-flip—she landed on the hard floor and fractured the bones at the balls of her feet where the toes connect.

After high school, she was recruited to play Division III soccer for Wittenberg University in Springfield, Ohio, and in her spare time joined the lacrosse team just for fun. This is a woman who likes to keep busy. "I get that from my dad," she says. "He is a Type A personality, very driven. His motto was, 'Do your best and have fun.'" Having an older brother also stoked her competitive nature. "Anything Steve did I did, and I wanted to do it better," she recalls. "I looked up to him and still do."

After college she moved to Wisconsin and joined a water-ski show team, the Min-Aqua-Bats, one of the oldest water-ski show teams in the United States. Her parents, both avid water-skiers, taught her the ropes at age seven. Her best event was water-skiing barefoot and forming pyramids with the other team members. She was a two-time national champion in the figure-eight endurance barefoot event.

An active life in sports doesn't come without its share of injuries. Once, while going about forty miles an hour barefooting, she attempted a trick but fell, almost breaking her back. She was taken out of the water strapped to a board and rushed to the hospital with violent muscle spasms. According to Remy, "There was a bunch more of other serious injuries, but that's just part of the nature of the sport. It never scared me."

Despite her injuries and high-level participation in sports, Remy is not a risk taker. She makes sure she is in condition to compete, doing circuit training, weight strengthening, and running to stay fit. "I don't ever want to be the weak link on a team, the one everyone has to wait for. That's not me," she explains. She met her husband Mike, now forty-nine, a former marine, while working as a counselor for the Hubert H. Humphrey Job Corps. He was also into fitness and showed her some new training techniques. "He still shows me new ways to work out and stay fit!" says Remy.

Remy and Mike eventually moved to Florida, where she got a teaching job at a local high school and coached cross-country, track, and soccer. She was never a runner, but learned how to coach and did every workout with the girls, even entering local 5K races. "I never asked anything of them that I couldn't do myself," says Remy. "Plus, I loved the challenge of doing something new."

When her first son, Quad, was born in 2005, she cut back on some of the coaching and finally gave it up in 2010 when Tien, her second son, was born. She kept up her running, entering 5Ks, 10Ks, and half-marathons, as well as dabbling in triathlons—but she never took to the cycling. In 2007 she ran a marathon, but it was made more challenging than she expected by the recurrence of an old hamstring injury from her water-skiing days—one in which she tore her hamstring almost off the bone during a ski-jumping accident. "I'm never doing that again," she vows.

So why would such a high-performing athlete want to take up a Tough Mudder? "I got bored with just running, and racing most weekends got expensive," she explains. "Our boys, nine and four, grow out of their clothes every couple of months, so I have to make financial choices."

When Brent Wilmot, her son's elementary school physical education teacher, suggested she and Mike join him in a Tough Mudder, she found her partner in crime. "He had me from the get-go," she recalls. "I said if Mike isn't interested, I certainly am." Like Remy and Mike, Wilmot was looking for the next sports craze and had an inkling this one would appeal to the couple. His hunch was right on the mark. The idea that Tough Mudder donates to Wounded Warrior appealed to Mike. They recruited another friend, Larry Cagle, described as a thrill seeker, to join. So the four of them signed up for the 2011 Tampa Tough Mudder.

They went into it like the blind leading the blind. They read the description online but that's about it. "This was something different, something fun," says Remy. "We were all in good shape so we didn't do anything training-wise."

Remy can describe every mile, every obstacle of her first OCR. "It was amazing, thrilling, my most exciting sporting event in years. Everything was new and so completely different from running races. I guess there's nothing like the first time! I will never forget how much fun we had," she says. From the moment they heard the opening motivational words, "the hype-you-up guy," and recited the Tough Mudder pledge, they were hooked. "Everyone is in the same boat, facing obstacles and helping each other. I love that," she says.

Thousands of participants split up into seventeen starting time groups staged from 8 a.m. to 1:20 p.m. Their team of four (they didn't have a name) stayed together. Mike found the obstacles similar to those he'd encountered in military training during his years in the marines. There was only one problem: Mike couldn't swim, something he had never disclosed to his wife. On the obstacle that required jumping from a fifteen-foot plank into ice water, they jumped together. After plunging deep into the cold water, Remy popped up and looked around for Mike. He finally surfaced but then quickly sank under. Between not knowing how to swim and the disorienting shock of the cold water, he passed out. Remy tried to hold him up but was struggling. A lifeguard jumped in and pulled him to shore. After a few minutes, he recovered and said he wanted to continue. "At first we were concerned, but when I knew he was fine, Wilmot and I got the laughing fits," she recalls. "How can a marine not know how to swim? How did I not know that after years of being married to him?" Good thing Mike has a sense of humor and is a trouper, going along with the laughs. In his second Tough Mudder, he got shocked so badly in his leg during the Electroshock Therapy obstacle that he lost the use of it; he went down in the mud and couldn't stand up. Remy recalls, "He looked like a fish out of water, flopping around in the mud trying to stand." She and Wilmot were not the only ones having a laugh at Mike's pain. The announcer got into the act and had a heyday describing Mike's condition to the spectators. Nothing is spared in a Tough Mudder. Not feelings, pain, or embarrassment. But Mike was in on the laugh as well, and laughed along through the pain.

When they finished, they were all elated. "I've had the runner's high, the water-skier's high, but this was the best high ever!" says Remy. And unlike a road race where you might just get a bagel and water at the finish, they were rewarded with the orange Tough Mudder headband, a protein bar, a beer, and a can of deodorant.

Since 2011 Remy and Wilmot have done Warrior Dashes, Savage events, and other obstacle course events. In March, she did her second Savage and first BattleFrog. Her kids did their first BattleFrog youth event. A Savage is half the distance of a Tough Mudder but the same number of obstacles: twenty-four or so. "That one was more strength challenging," she adds.

Remy and Wilmot, whom she refers to as her mud racing partner, are already signed up for their fifth Tough Mudder in Palm Bay, Florida. She recruits other friends to join her and Wilmot in their passion for OCRs. Every year, they get together a team of newbies and train them. Some years the team has had twenty-four members. "Starting a few months out from the event, we do team training to motivate them. As they form friendships you can see the camaraderie building, which is so important because OCRs are all about teamwork. It's also fun for us as we are all teachers and love sharing our knowledge and techniques with others," says Remy. "We stick together—no team member left behind!"

She also gets her girlfriends involved. Her idea of a girls' weekend away is Prison Break paintball. As she describes it: "A lot of mud was involved. It was a four-mile course through woods dodging paintball snipers, at which I did not fare well. I ate a paintball ten minutes in and my lower lip was big as a hot dog by the end with a bit of bloodshed. The girls and I were first in line for the beer tent."

She keeps her Tough Mudder headbands hanging on the rearview mirror of her car. "They make me smile," she says. "And every so often I'll be at a stoplight and a car will pull up next to me and the driver has a Tough Mudder headband hanging on their rearview mirror. That's a kick." She even has a Tough Mudder nickname, Mud Nut. Mike is Big Mike. And there's Gladiator, a co-worker of Remy's who also works at Universal Studios as an actor playing parts like the Exterminator. He's famous for his Halloween night horror roles, stilt walking, and more. All of which begs the question: Do OCRs attract a crazy crowd?

Remy would like to branch out and do Tough Mudders in national locations, but with two kids and a full-time job it isn't in the plans or the budget just yet. Her long-term goal is to qualify for the World's Toughest Mudder; for now, though, she's content doing one Tough Mudder a year and a few Warrior Dashes with her newbie teams just for fun. "Warrior Dashes are great for first-timers," she says. "It's only a 5K course, the obstacles aren't as challenging as a Tough Mudder, and it's a complete party atmosphere."

Remy truly is a Mud Nut. Obstacle course races fit perfectly into her life; they don't take as much time as a marathon, they can be enjoyed with friends, and there is always a party afterward. She's gotten her husband and kids involved so it has become a family event. Remy is living life to the fullest, and OCRs are a part of it. This former barefoot water-skier, who still barefoots whenever she gets the chance, wouldn't have it any other way. She always seems to land on her feet.

MIKE WILLIAMS

49, Ocoee, Florida

"My wife is crazy. I just follow her lead."

Now we get to hear Mike's side of the story. Did this former marine really not know how to swim? Why did he sign up for a Tough Mudder?

"I just follow my wife. She's crazy and gets me to do these crazy things," says Williams, aka Big Mike. But he has his own crazy past. Both his parents were in the army—in fact, he is the fourth generation of the Williams family to serve in the military. He joined the marines in 1983, against the wishes of his mother, an army transportation specialist. "She thought the marines were crazy and wanted me to go into the army," says Williams. "But it was the best thing I ever did." There are three things the military does well, and Williams has more than his share of discipline, loyalty, and integrity.

The marines love their sports, and when they found out that Williams was a former high school football star, they signed him up to play for his battalion. When he wasn't doing his job as a logistics specialist, he was wining games for them. After four years of active duty, Williams received a football scholarship to play at Huron University in South Dakota. At six feet tall, slender, and a former eight-hundred-meter runner, he made the perfect quarterback. Upon graduation he continued his football career in Germany playing for a German-American football team. "I loved my three years playing in Europe," he says. "The history was amazing. Our hometown stadium in Nuremberg is where Hitler used to give his propaganda speeches."

Coming back to the States in 1995, he joined the Hubert Humphrey Job Corps in St. Paul, Minnesota, which is where he met Remy. They married in 2003 and moved to Florida, where he is now the assistant regional director of security for Westgate Resorts.

In some ways, Williams never left the marines. He was officially discharged in 1991 but lives by the motto, "Once a marine, always a marine." He works out five to six times a week with weights, CrossFit, pickup ball games, and now "the crazy obstacle course racing my wife has me doing," he says. "I go along with it. For me, it's like boot camp all over again." He felt he didn't need to train for the first one he did with Remy and Wilmot. About the only preparation he did was to go online and look at the obstacles. "I have to admit I was not thrilled when I read about the Electroshock Therapy," he says, "but everything else seemed like being back in the marines."

He describes the Tough Mudder as running a little, climbing over or under things, getting muddy, and scaling walls. When he got to the obstacle that Remy described as Mike almost drowning, he wants to add his two cents: "I do know how to swim! Let me just put that out there. I may not be the best swimmer, but I can survive in the water. Remy jumped first, then I jumped. The water was freezing, and deep. As I surfaced, I felt things lock up. I must have looked bad because Remy took one look at me and asked if I was all right. I said no, and then sank! I was pulled out of the water and to the side, but really, I was fine. I just needed a few seconds to recover. It was a bit comical. As soon as Remy knew I was all right, she started laughing at the fact that I sank like a stone." He was back on the course in no time. "No time to rest, I had to keep up with Remy and Wilmot," says Mike.

That's not the last time Mike did something that caused a few ripples of laughter from the crowd. In his second Tough Mudder he got nailed in Electroshock Therapy. As he recalls: "It's always one of the last obstacles so I knew it was coming. Remy and the rest of our team were ahead of me. I was almost through when I got hit with a bolt of electricity that sent me facedown in the mud. I couldn't even stand up, the pain was so bad. It totally locked up my calf muscle. I was flailing in the mud like a fish out of water and all I could hear was the announcer and my wife laughing hysterically. I started laughing as well because I knew how pathetic I must have looked." Good thing he has a sense of humor.

Since that second one, Mike now prefers to watch his wife compete. He does understand the appeal of OCRs: "I think it's the unknown factor. In most every other sport you know what's happening, what to expect. When I'm playing football, I may call a different play but basically the goal is the same—move the ball down the field for a touchdown. Same in running. Just run down the miles. But in an OCR, there is always the unexpected, a surprise obstacle that throws you for a loop. I think people like that element of surprise."

The bigger appeal for this former marine was the tie-in with the Wounded Warrior Project. "This was very important to me," says Williams. "With my family background in the military and my friends in the marines, I wanted to show my respect and support for the Wounded Warriors. It feels good to do something that's more important than just doing it for myself."

Williams has also found that OCRs have become part of their family lifestyle. For him, exercise is as natural as breathing. He's up at 5 a.m. to get his workout in, and then Remy goes out for her exercise so someone is always there for the kids. And speaking of the kids, they embrace the exercise lifestyle as well. "They love doing the Tough Mudder kids' races," says Williams. "I feel very blessed."

ADVICE FROM THE PROS:

Alex Nicholas, EPIC Hybrid Training, Manhattan, New York, and Miami, Florida

Alex Nicholas, a former member of the Reebok Spartan Pro Team, has a fitness résumé that includes countless race podium finishes from Spartans to duathlons; two appearances on *American Ninja Warrior*; and founding and owning EPIC Hybrid Training in New York City. Nicholas likes a challenge, and it seems he has never met one he couldn't accept.

Nicholas got involved with OCRs by accident. He was looking up the movie *300* online and an ad for a Spartan Race popped up. It was love at first sight. "I read the ad and thought, *This is so cool!*" says Nicholas. Everything about it appealed to his inner athlete. He ran track and played basketball in high school, and played football at the University of Delaware. He then took up martial arts. He did his first Spartan Sprint in 2012 in Tuxedo and placed in the top ten. He won his next one in Fenway Park, Boston, against a field of five thousand, calling it one of his most memorable moments.

Not only did he get hooked, he was tapped to be a member of the first Spartan Pro Team in 2013. In that role, he was part pro, part trainer. One of his most inspiring Spartan clients who went on to be a close friend is Amanda Sullivan. He was at her side for many Spartan events, including her Spartan Beast in Texas in 2014. "Alex was the only person I knew I wanted at my side for the Beast," says Sullivan. "No one can do what he does." After two years of traveling the country with Spartan and helping to put the series on the map, he retired from the pro team to dedicate more time to his EPIC enterprise in Manhattan and opening franchises in Miami. "When the opportunity calls, you answer," says Nicholas.

EPIC, described as the toughest exercise class in the city by the *New York Daily News*, is his baby. He created it in part as a response to the obstacle course racing craze, adding high-intensity interval and circuit-based training, ideal for Spartan races. "Spartan will test you," says Nicholas. "You've really got to be an all-around good athlete and pay attention to all parts of your physical fitness to do well. And if you think you can do an endurance race because you've run a marathon, think again. This is a whole new adventure." He firmly believes that doing crosstraining and adding weight strengthening is critical to OCR training. He uses a lot of kettle bells in his workouts, which add agility, stability, and coordination.

As a trainer, he doesn't believe in the drill sergeant method or yelling at his clients. He's encouraging, motivational, but doesn't suffer laziness or excuses. Here is how Nicholas approaches new clients thinking about doing an OCR:

First Question: What Is Your Goal?

1. To say you did it.

2. To finish with your pride intact and a smile.

3. To compete with a finish time in mind.

Second Question: How Much Time Do You Have to Train?

Ideally, twelve weeks is perfect. But if you only have a week, there are still things you can do. What you want to avoid is not being prepared at all. You don't want this to be a miserable experience because you didn't put in any time.

The Basics

1. Get in some running, especially trail running. You have to get to the next obstacle. If you can't do an obstacle, you can do a Burpee—but you have to get there first. Do trail hikes, especially inclines. Practice going downhill and running on uneven terrain. Research where the event is taking place. Most Spartan events are on ski slopes, which can be treacherous; you'll be running down trails with rocks and roots and loose stones everywhere.

2. Practice Burpees. These are the single greatest full-body exercise, building endurance, strength, and overall fitness. Start with five a day and add one a day till you get to thirty a day.

3. Rope climbs. You can count on doing a number of rope climbs. Practice the different ways to climb a rope and see what works best for you. There's a J-hook method and an S-hook method. Google them.

The Must-Haves

Confidence! You need to believe you can do this. Even the pros get butterflies before an event.

Best Fit Tip

Get outside your comfort zone! Don't be afraid to try different workouts and explore new routines!

ADVICE FROM THE PROS:

Rob Jaroszuk, RISE Fitness, Ho-Ho-Kus, New Jersey

Founder and owner of RISE Fitness, Rob Jaroszuk holds a WITS certificate in personal and group training, Sandbag certificate, Vipr certificate, TRX certificate, Certificate Level 1 MoveNat, and FMS. He is a graduate of the Navy SEAL Leadership Under Fire Redux (Coronado, California, 2013) and has trained clients for Ninja Warrior and obstacle course races.

"This is not a test," he says of doing OCRs. He starts out his training sessions with a basic question: "What do you want to accomplish? It's important to know what the participant's goal is before setting out a training plan. Do they want to destroy the course or just finish?"

Think Out the Entire Training Program

A lot of variables go into a training plan besides conditioning and strength training. One is weather. If the event is in summer, it's important to practice staying hydrated in the heat in case there are no fluid stations on the course. If the event is in the fall or winter, he suggests training in the cold and getting used to wearing gear that will stave off hypothermia, which can happen with all the water and mud obstacles. "Long pants, long-sleeved shirts, both made of wicking fabric, is key to staying warm," he advises. "Hats, gloves, boots, anything to keep you warm." Both cold and heat can make you miserable and derail your performance if you are not prepared.

Here are a few of Jaroszuk's tips for completing an OCR.

Do Your Research

Go online and look up your event. Most sites offer a glimpse of the course and many of its obstacles. Learn what obstacles you most likely will face and figure out how you would do it. YouTube offers many videos of OCR obstacles and how to conquer them. Do as much research as possible so you can better devise your training plan. Where is the event taking place? What is the terrain? What is the predicted weather?

Training

If you have access to a gym or a trainer, and the budget to afford that, it's the best way to go. But if you don't, you can still get in shape.

1. Get outside and find your own obstacle course. Use the monkey bars at a playground. Do pull-ups on the bars. Go to a beach and crawl through the sand. Make sandbags and carry them through the parking lot.

2. Run outside, especially on trails. Run on uneven surfaces. Carry logs, even a training partner, for at least a tenth of a mile. This will train you in how to carry heavy objects as well as engaging more core muscles.

3. Upper-body strength is key. Obstacles that require upper-body strength are the toughest for most of the participants. Practice on cargo nets, scale walls, do pull-ups, planks, and lateral pull-downs.

4. Practice balancing. Walk on a slack line or a two-inch balance beam. Stand on a single leg and do curls or shoulder presses with dumbbells.

5. Commit yourself to a training schedule and be consistent in your training. Build up your endurance. The more you improve your conditioning, the more you decrease the chances of getting injured.

Do It with a Team

Most OCRs are designed to be done with a team. Teammates help one another through the obstacles and share a bond of empowerment and camaraderie. But the team concept can backfire if there is a speedy member and a slow one who become at odds with each other. After waiting at a few obstacles for everyone else, the faster members can get aggravated. In cold weather, they risk hypothermia while they wait; in the heat, they risk cramping. Some may also be competitive and feel held back. The best policy is to be open and honest, addressing these points and any other concerns as a team. If you have a large group, you may want to break it up into three subgroups: slow, medium, and fast.

Sleep

No one expects a car to go far on a nearly empty tank. Yet people demand great performance from their body on an empty sleep tank. Get enough rest, which also helps to restore muscles depleted from all the training. Everyone feels better and performs better when fully charged.

The Must-Haves

Be well balanced in mind and body. They work together. Feed your mind with positive and empowering beliefs. Feed your body with balanced portions of rest, training, and the right intensity for your goal.

Best Fit Tip

The event is the icing on the cake after all the hard training preparing for it. The journey is about what you learn along the way in the process of reaching of your goal. Celebrate it and have a blast.

Conclusion: I Got Muddy

I owe a huge debt of thanks to Alex Nicholas, who shamed me into doing a Spartan Sprint. When I told him I hadn't done an OCR yet, he said I needed to experience one if I was going to write about them. He was right. And doing it with Don Kannenberg, who coached and supported me through the obstacles, was the only way I could have even attempted one. The five-thousand-plus participants came in all shapes and sizes. They were mostly in the twenty-to-thirty age range, but everyone was welcomed.

Tips

1. Don't wear any jewelry, especially earrings or necklaces that can get caught in barbed wire. Makeup is optional.

2. Tie back any loose hair that can get in the way or get caught in barbed wire.

3. Think about adding sports gloves and arm sleeves to your gear for protection in climbing and crawling.

4. Think about your phobias. Are you claustrophobic? Afraid of

heights? Know before you go.

5. Safety first. Don't be a hero. Take your time and watch your footing, especially on the downhills where the trails can be slippery and treacherous.

6. Study the obstacle before proceeding. If you haven't done it already, go online to watch videos of obstacles and how participants handled them. If you haven't done that, watch other participants get through an obstacle before you attempt it. And rely on the support and help of the volunteers and others.

Recovery

It might be time for your first ice bath. I had lots of black-and-blue bruises on my legs and arms, mostly from the Barbed Wire Crawl. The other parts of my body were sore and achy from the stress of the downhill running and climbing over walls. Taking a ten-minute ice bath helps to alleviate the soreness and helps muscles recover faster. Take one as soon as you get home.

The Cleanup

My clothes were disgusting after crawling through mud all morning. And smelly, really gross. Most events have showers for rinsing off layers of mud and blood and a bin for throwaway clothes and gear if you can't stand the thought of taking them home. I changed my top but wish I had changed out of my capris—the car reeked. I threw them out as soon as I got home. Don Kannenberg stashes his muddy gear in a plastic bag. When he gets home he lays his clothes and gear on the lawn, sprays them down with a hose, and then decides what to keep and what to trash.

A Long Shower

It took me forever to scrub away the mud. After toweling off, I used a Q-tip for my ears, behind the ears, and my nostrils. Mud gets into places you can't even imagine, so don't rush through your personal hygiene. And brush your teeth: Grit gets lodged in your mouth.

The Takeaway

What I remember most from my Spartan Sprint was the kindness of strangers and the helping hands that seemingly came out of nowhere to help me over an obstacle or pull barbed wire out of my shirt. The constant "You got it, girl!" and "Looking good" (how can you look good covered in mud?) was music to my ears and appreciated. And someone said I had booty! I've never had a booty call before in my life, but I was happy to accept it during the Barbed Wire Crawl.

When I was climbing the A-Frame Cargo Net, scared out of mind and frozen in midair, Don was on one side calming me down, telling me exactly where to place my foot to move forward. Then I heard from behind me, "Don't worry. I got your back," and then from the side, "I'm here, too," from strangers who recognized a first-timer who didn't have a clue what to do and took their time to make sure I got over the net and down. That happened throughout the course and is a trademark of most OCRs. It truly takes a team to get through it, unless you are in the elite field and looking to collect the winner's purse and stand on the podium. As I continued on the course I constantly heard friends calling for their friends, waiting for them, or encouraging them.

CONCLUSION
I Got Muddy

As Alex suggested, I got it. I now understand the lure of OCRs and why people do them, whether it's "one and done" or they transform you into an OCR fanatic or the occasional weekend warrior. People who do OCRs are sometimes referred to as "crazy." I asked Joe DeSena if he agreed with that. He responded, "People who do OCRs aren't crazy, they are alive!" He continued, "These are people who are looking for something more out of life, to shake up their life even for a day." It definitely shook up my life for a day, and judging from the party atmosphere that continued as participants finished the course, I would have to say that they felt pretty stoked.

Too many people go through life restricting themselves to the easy, well-worn path. It's safe, it's familiar, and it's non-threatening. But if you want to discover something about yourself, to see how deep you can dig and overcome obstacles, not just on a course but throughout life, then you just might want to sign up for an OCR. Yes, you'll get muddy, but you will also come away knowing you accomplished the impossible. That feeling will last a lifetime.

ACKNOWLEDGMENTS

When my publisher, Garth Battista of Breakaway Books, called to suggest I write a book on obstacle course racing, I wasn't sure. I had covered the first World's Toughest Mudder in Englishtown, New Jersey, in December 2012 for *Marathon and Beyond* magazine, and although I admired the determination of the participants I also thought they were crazy. With temperatures plunging into the twenties and wind-chills into single digits, the twenty-four-hour endurance test left 90 percent of the field in the medical tent shivering with hypothermia. Nothing about this event appealed to my marathoner mind-set.

But I have seen the light and am now a believer in all things OCR. After interviewing the athletes in *Get Muddy*, everyone from the coach potatoes to the pros, I have nothing but the utmost respect and admiration for all of them. I owe a great deal of thanks to everyone who opened their lives to me and explained in sometimes embarrassing detail how they survived their first obstacle course race. Over phone interviews we laughed, cried, and shared emotional moments—and I discovered a new world of driven, determined, gutsy, and most of all fun people. And crazy. I still remember the pause in my conversation with Victor Cotto when he told me he'd trained for his first Spartan race by chopping down a tree. I didn't quite know how to follow up with that. When the amazing Amanda Sullivan and I discovered we were both Jersey girls, a bond formed. When she sent me a photo of herself with Bruce Springsteen, who'd invited her to his house for lunch with her boyfriend Todd Love, she instantly became Jersey royalty. Melinda and Eryk Collings described in detail how they formerly drank liters of Mountain Dew and smoked a pack of cigarettes a day while ignoring the image in the mirror creeping upward in weight till Eryk was pushing three hundred pounds. Their wake-up call was doing a Warrior Dash, which changed their lives. They gave up their cable TV subscription to pay for a gym membership to train for the event, then never went back to watching television.

Dave Huckle of Weeple Army and I spent mornings on the phone together while he drove to work. It was the only free time he had to do an interview. Not only was Dave generous with his time, but he also introduced me to other people; all it took was me saying, "Dave suggested I speak with you," to open doors. Dave has single-handedly done so much to create a welcoming and fun community for people of all levels to join and embrace OCRs. Alex Nicholas, former OCR pro and trainer, introduced me to my first OCR and to Joe DeSena. He is a true ambassador of the sport. And what a thrill to interview Margaret Schlachter, a pioneer of OCR and the first professional female obstacle course racer.

I owe a huge thanks to Lauren Gardner of Red Frog Events, which puts on Warrior Dash, and Denise Mast with Spartan Race, Inc. They were not only helpful in opening doors to the pros and other great people, but checked in with me every few weeks to see how I was doing—despite being in their busiest season while I was searching for profiles for *Get Muddy*. Lauren and Denise see firsthand how completing just one OCR can transform lives.

I also want to thank my friends who reached out to their friends and started a network of people who have done OCRs. Friends truly are the best resources for anything in life. If it weren't for Don Kannenberg dragging me onto the course of my first Spartan Sprint, I never would have experienced the thrill of an OCR.

Finally, I want to acknowledge anyone who has ever taken that first step—the hardest one—to start a journey that will change their lives and set them free of self-doubt. As Randy Pierce, the first American blind person to complete a Tough Mudder, says: "Believing you *can* is the first step." Every underdog, underachieving, overweight, or scared first-timer who finds the courage to toe any starting line in life will cross that finish line with a new confidence, a sense of empowerment, and the belief that they can accomplish anything.

GLOSSARY

Burpees: The Burpee is a full-body exercise. Begin in a standing position.

1. Drop into a position with your hands on the ground.

2. Kick your feet back, while keeping your arms extended..

3. Do a push-up.

4. Immediately return your feet to the squat position.

5. Jump up from the squat position.

CrossFit: CrossFit, Inc., is a fitness company founded by Greg Glassman and Lauren Jenai in 2000 and promoted as both a physical exercise philosophy and a competitive fitness sport. CrossFit workouts incorporate elements from high-intensity interval training, Olympic weight lifting, plyometrics, power lifting, gymnastics, calisthenics, strongman, and other exercises.

Dri-Fit fabric: Moisture-wicking fabric is commonly used in work-out clothing and sportswear. The material is designed to pull sweat and perspiration off the skin and out to the exterior of the fabric. Moisture-wicking fabric can also be important in the prevention of hypothermia.

GoRuck bag: GoRuck gear is designed by a former Green Beret and made in the USA to withstand the harshest conditions. GoRuck gear range from hydration systems to backpacks, gloves, and clothing (goruck.com).

GoRuck event: An event where participants put weights on their backs and go for a walk. More weight or more miles equals more results (goruck.com).

Weeple Army: Founded by Dave Huckle as a community for OCR participants—from first-timers to advanced athletes—to have fun while participating in events, Weeple Army now offers training and other resources:

www.weeplearmy.com

www.facebook.com/groups/WeepleArmy

RESOURCES

With the exception of some training books, most of the resources for OCRs are available online. It can be argued that obstacle course racing is the first sport to come of age in the digital era. The major organizers publish their own online magazines. Every series, every obstacle, every event can be found on the web. YouTube has hundreds of videos of the courses, obstacles, and training techniques.

Books

Obstacle Race Training: How to Beat Any Course, Compete Like a Champion and Change Your Life by Margaret Schlachter, Tuttle Publishing.

Ultimate Obstacle Race Training by Brett Stewart, Ulysses Press.

Spartan Up! by Joe DeSena, Houghton Mifflin Harcourt Publishing.

Online

MudRunGuide.com: Brett Stewart's website dedicated to everything OCR

ObstacleRacingMedia.com

Obstacleracing.about.com

Mudandadventure.com

Mudrunfun.com

OCR Warrior

Obstacle and Adventure Weekly

Videos

Amanda Sullivan: https://www.facebook.com/AmandaSullivanSmiles/videos/44655100214

Randy Pierce: http://heroes.oberto.com/randy

Misty Diaz: www.youtube.com/watch?v=gITvm7Uf1Vo

Other titles of interest from Breakaway Books

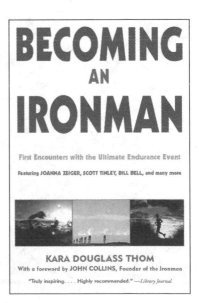

RUNNING THROUGH THE WALL
Personal Encounters With the Ultramarathon

Featuring stories by
ANN TRASON
TIM TWIETMEYER
DAVID HORTON
IAN TORRENCE
and many more

Foreword by
DON ALLISON,
UltraRunning Magazine

Neal Jamison

ZENDURANCE

A Spiritual Fitness Guide for Endurance Athletes

Shane Alton Eversfield
With a foreword by Paula Newby-Fraser

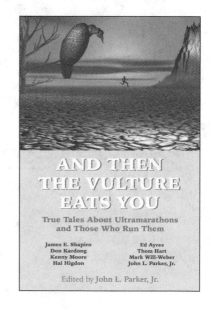

THE
RUNNER'S
HIGH

illumination and ecstasy in motion

AND THEN
THE VULTURE
EATS YOU

True Tales About Ultramarathons
and Those Who Run Them

James E. Shapiro   Ed Ayres
Don Kardong   Thom Hart
Kenny Moore   Mark Will-Weber
Hal Higdon   John L. Parker, Jr.

Edited by John L. Parker, Jr.